PRESSURE POINTS

the chief executive press

PRESSURE POINTS

ROBERT W. LEAR

whittle direct books

Photographs: Henry M. Minton and Dwight C. Minton, courtesy of D.C. Minton, page 15;
Dwight C. Minton by Sylvia Plachy, page 15; Robert E. Flynn by David Blachman,
courtesy of the Juvenile Diabetes Foundation, page 51; Cyril C. Baldwin Jr. and
Arthur I. Mendolia, courtesy of the Cambrex Corporation, page 77; David
T. Kearns by T. Michael Keza/ © Nation's Business, page 83.

The Chief Executive Press: Dorothy Foltz-Gray, Senior Editor;
Ken Smith, Design Director; Evelyn Ellis, Art Director

Library of Congress Catalog Card Number: 92-61351
Lear, Robert W.
Pressure Points
ISBN 1- 879736-10-1
ISSN 1060-8923

the chief executive press

The Chief Executive Press presents original short books by distinguished authors on subjects of special importance to the topmost executives of the world's major businesses.

The series is edited and published by Whittle Books, a business unit of Whittle Communications L.P. Books appear several times a year, and the series reflects a broad spectrum of responsible opinions. In each book the opinions expressed are those of the author, not the publisher or the advertiser.

I welcome your comments on this ambitious endeavor.

William S. Rukeyser
Editor in Chief

This book is dedicated to my wife, Dorothy Lear,
to my sons, William and Andrew,
and to my daughter-in-law, Patricia.

C O N T E N T S

FOREWORD

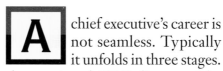chief executive's career is not seamless. Typically it unfolds in three stages.

In Stage One the newly appointed CEO discovers the power and glory of his job. He dives into his work, focusing his energy on the company's problems and opportunities. He meets with his people, organizes his work, and learns the business of being CEO. It can be and usually is a wonderfully productive period. But a CEO can stay so busy in Stage One that he becomes enmeshed in corporate trivia, and so impressed by his ability to handle decisions that he fails to keep his company abreast of changing times.

In Stage Two the chief executive discovers his fellow CEOs. He becomes aware of intriguing extracurricular activities: outside boards, trade association meetings, CEO gatherings, and community programs. When this stage is properly handled, a CEO can learn from his fellow CEOs much that is useful to him and his company. Sometimes, however, he can get caught up in so many outside boards and meetings that he becomes a partial CEO.

In the third stage the CEO discovers the world outside

the corporate community. As a prelude to retirement he becomes less active in detailed company matters and more interested in external affairs—charitable, political, academic, social, economic. If his succession plan is in place and his organization is functioning well, a wise CEO can contribute effectively to his company *and* to society during this period. But sometimes a CEO in Stage Three becomes so deluded by self-importance that he can't be bothered with corporate problems. He gets out of touch with his people, products, processes, customers, competition, and, sadly, with reality. His board looks forward to his retirement and, as we are seeing more frequently, may hasten the process.

While these three stages are quite normal to pass through, they may not be clearly defined. The definition of each stage is cloudy and the line of demarcation between stages murky. A CEO doesn't suddenly move from one stage to begin another. There is much sloshing through the marshes before the Rubicon is crossed, followed by more sloshing. But virtually all CEOs who stay on the job long enough pass through these stages.

A number of CEOs make the passages happily, keeping themselves under control. I know others who lost their perspective in one or more of the stages, but not to an extreme degree. And distressingly, I know some who lost their balance so badly that they also lost their jobs.

These observations—based upon my own experiences as a CEO, a board director, and for the past 15 years as executive-in-residence at Columbia Business School—formed the basis of an article I wrote for *Chief Executive* magazine in August 1991 titled "The Three Stages of a CEO."

Once I began researching these stages, I found that they had been a target area of research and writing by academic observers for several years. In particular, Professor Donald Hambrick of Columbia Business School had written a paper for the 1991 *Academy of Management Review* titled "The Seasons of a CEO's Tenure."

Tony Kiser of Whittle Books read my article and asked me to expand the concept into a book. As a result I talked with a broad range of CEOs, asking them if they agreed with my three-stage concept and, if so, what they do or have done to stay in balance.

In general my CEO sources agreed with my concept of three stages. Most averred that they had never left Stage One, but they all knew *other* CEOs who had lost their balance in at least two of the stages.

When I asked them to tell me how they kept steady, I did not get a single clear answer. They explained that they were different and their companies were different. They talked about hard work, being in the right place at the right time, not being exposed to undue temptation, and so on.

Woven through their comments was the undercurrent of a personal plan, or an agenda. Not always a written document—or at least not a formal one—a personal plan was more an idea or timetable indicating where the CEO would like to be and when, but with much built-in flexibility to accommodate inevitable changes.

When I asked them whom they went to for advice and help with their personal planning, again they had no standard response. Many, perhaps most, kept concerns to themselves and faced the uncharted waters without benefit of professional counsel. A few found mentors among their directors and business associates, but most of the time they were on their own.

What surprised me, however, was their interest and willingness to talk about their experiences and about their observations of other CEOs. Only rarely did a CEO tell me that he was adequately prepared at the outset for the complexity, the demands, and the stress of his job. Because they had seen other CEOs in operation, they *thought* they knew what was coming. But they didn't know until it came.

What can be done to help you move through the various stages confident that you can maintain your balance? What does it take to be an effective chief executive throughout your career?

Certainly it's helpful to know in advance that there are definite stages and to recognize the symptoms and pitfalls of each. All professionals do this—golfers, soldiers, gardeners, movie directors. They plot their course, anticipate problems, and look for opportunity. They also seek the best advice they can get from those who know the course.

I am indebted to Tony Kiser and Dorothy Foltz-Gray of Whittle Books, who have patiently guided me through the research and writing of this book; to J. P. Donlon, editor of *Chief Executive* magazine, who was a great help in reviewing my manuscript; and most of all to the dozens of CEOs, directors, and CEO watchers who have so generously given me their time and thoughts about the three stages of a CEO.

One small but special point. I know that there are female CEOs, and many more are on the way. Right now, however, well over 99 percent of all corporate CEOs are men, so in referring here to a CEO, I use the pronoun *he*. I ask my readers and my M.B.A. students at Columbia Business School to forgive me.

It is no secret that customer service has become increasingly important to the success of every business, but in aviation the ability to respond promptly and effectively is absolutely essential.

That's why customer service at Cessna begins early in the process of developing each new aircraft.

We listen carefully to our customers with respect to component and systems reliability, and we recognize that minimizing both aircraft downtime and the cost of maintenance are exceedingly high priorities.

Comprehensive product support agreements are required of every vendor, and intensive fatigue testing continues long after the aircraft is certified. It is not surprising, then, that Citations are the most reliable business jets in the world.

And when service is needed, Cessna is the only aircraft manufacturer which provides factory-direct support through a network of company-owned Citation Service Centers.

This service organization is augmented by factory-appointed Citation Service Stations strategically located throughout the world. Backing up this service network is a parts distribution and hot line system that provides 24-hour-a-day, 7-day-a-week availability.

Citation business jets provide by far the most efficient and effective air transportation for an increasing number of companies. Therefore, we are committed at Cessna to assuring that every Citation is ready to dispatch when called upon.

Obviously, this commitment requires exceptional customer support and that's one of our most important goals.

Sincerely yours,

Russell W. Meyer, Jr.
Chairman and Chief Executive Officer
Cessna Aircraft Company

Cessna Aircraft Company · One Cessna Boulevard · Wichita, Kansas 67215 · 316/941-7400

Cessna
A Textron Company

Chapter One

STAGE ONE: THE CEO DISCOVERS HIMSELF

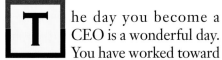

he day you become a CEO is a wonderful day. You have worked toward this day for as long as 40 years. You have overcome great obstacles, taken much risk, and competed head-on with many rivals. You have attended a thousand meetings, taken hundreds of trips, written countless memos, and reported to dozens of bosses. You have been a trainee, a supervisor, and a vice-president. You may have been president and chief operating officer or vice-chairman.

You have been around the block.

Now you are gaining recognition for your hard work, respect for your managerial ability, and acknowledgment for your leadership. You are also lucky, for you have caught the eye of the right people at the right time.

You have won the top job in the company. The chairman and the retiring CEO have told you of your election by the board, and compliments follow. You telephone your wife and family, and glowing press releases go out. There has been a coronation ceremony. Your picture will be in the newspapers tomorrow and in the trade magazines next month.

You are the new boss. As the new CEO, you have immediate access to all of the power and perquisites of that office. There is no place to hide; the spotlight follows you wherever you go. You represent the company. You *are* the company.

Have you achieved success? Not yet. It is, as Winston Churchill said, "the end of the beginning."

Starting Off

The last thing you are thinking about is your entrance into a multistage situation. Far from it. You are champing at the bit to move into your new office and lead the company.

You look forward to your first board meeting as CEO, and you know that all eyes will be watching to see how you handle yourself. Your board may name you chairman or offer you all three titles: chairman, president, and chief executive officer. At this point you probably don't care too much as long as you are the CEO.

You eagerly anticipate your first management meeting as top dog. Although you may have been the president and chief operating officer before, you were not the CEO. Now you are, and everyone in the company recognizes the significance. As you walk up the steps to applause, you get a shiver up your spine like you have never had before.

You are off on a great adventure—the discovery of your power and the glory of exercising it. If you use that power thoughtfully, you can have a wonderful time. But if you do not have a road map, you can waste time and may even lose your way.

You begin making lists of what you want to do in the next few weeks: places to go, people to see, projects to start, changes to make. You know, of course, that things will be different. You will have more responsibility, new privileges, and your risk-to-reward ratio will shift.

The differences show up quickly. The brighter smiles, the firmer handshakes, the respectful voices. You get mounds of congratulatory letters from people you barely know. People ask you questions and, surprisingly, listen to your answers. "Hmmm," you say, "they never did that before."

You may think *you* haven't changed, but your surroundings have. And no matter how valiantly you resist it, you will begin to change too.

One of the first tasks is moving into your new office—usually the retiring CEO's big corner space. You do a little renovating—from rebuilding to personalizing with pictures and mementos. Almost always the new CEO makes it clear that this is *his* office. An absolute change has been made.

Many CEOs use the opportunity to illustrate a new managerial style; indeed, some CEOs have built entirely new office buildings. In any case your new office makes a statement. If the former CEO was old-fashioned and conservative, you switch to modern furniture, add a computer terminal, plug in a stock-quote machine, and hang contemporary art. If the former CEO was a spendthrift, you set the pace with smaller space and plain furnishings. If he was revered and is still around, the changes can wait.

The secretarial setup also sends a message. The new CEO may move along his present secretary, shift to another senior secretary, or inject an outsider with an English accent and the title of executive secretary. Only rarely, however, does the incoming CEO take over the outgoing CEO's secretary; that is too much identification with an earlier regime.

Some trappings are automatic. The parking space. A chauffeured limousine or company car. A private restroom and shower. A WATS line and fax machine at home. An executive dining room (which provides lots of other ways to show off a new managerial style). That joy of all corporate joys, the company plane.

And no self-respecting CEO can operate without the backup of a club or two. Many senior executives are entitled to company-paid memberships in a luncheon club and a country club. And the CEO title often leads to a more lofty club where the big hitters congregate. It may be the Milwaukee Club, the Petroleum Club of Houston, the Duquesne Club in Pittsburgh, or the Pacific-Union Club in San Francisco. For golf, it may be Cypress Point at Monterey, the National at Southhampton, Blind Brook in New York, or the holy of holies, the National at Augusta. It's a landmark day when a senior board member calls to say, "Can you have lunch with me on Thursday? I want to introduce you to the chairman of our club's membership committee."

Other things fall into place. As CEO you automatically become your company's senior representative at the industry trade association. You sit on the dais at all kinds of banquets. You conduct the annual meeting, meet the press, greet distinguished visitors, and get lots of mail.

Invariably, inevitably, you begin to adapt. You buy a few new suits—some jazzy Armani togs or English custom tailoring. You start wearing Turnbull & Asser shirts with white collars, striped bodies, and big cuff links. You may even think about having your hair styled and your face lifted. "After all," you say, "if one is going to be in the public eye..."

To be sure, many new CEOs are only minimally affected by the trappings. In certain company cultures, under austere circumstances or where the management successor is a clone or has long been heir apparent, the transition is barely noticeable. Indeed, the goal may be to make things seem the same. But no new CEO can resist adding his own imprint.

Despite the distractions of settling into a new office with your new toys, you must buckle down to a whirlwind of activities. And you do. You work hard. For a while you are one of the first in and the last to leave. This is not surprising, for one of the traits that got you the job was your ability to outwork your peers. And there are so many people to meet, there is so much to read, so long a checklist; you rush out of the chute.

You meet your people. Everyone wants to greet you or, if they know you, to congratulate you, and, unless you have been brought in to rip the place apart, you enjoy the process. You visit each office and shake hands with everyone. You give speeches, hold luncheons, and may even cut a video tape. You are not ready to make pronouncements of policy or change, but you reaffirm your respect for the company and its employees and pledge to work on the problems and opportunities. This is effective, for frequently it has been months since the workers have seen their CEO.

You call on key customers, suppliers, distributors, dealers. As CEO you have access to the CEOs or senior executives of your customers, and you capitalize on it. Your salesmen and agents are delighted. You learn about your company's competitiveness, its service, its quality, its prices, and its image. From your suppliers you find out what other companies do to improve costs and efficiency. You quiz your distributors and dealers about how to improve the company's market share. You take pages and pages of notes. You follow up.

You sit in on meetings throughout the company. Some you call and chair yourself. Many are routine division and department meetings that you attend to show your interest and concern. A few are special meetings to brief you on existing programs. People are astonished at your attention span and your bladder control.

You find out how things are done. You look into management information services, legal backlogs, quality procedures, performance reviews, succession tables, bonus plans, audit reports—the whole bottomless pit of things that you need to know about and change.

You appoint task forces and project teams to look into decisions held open for your review. You spend lots of time choosing these groups and reading their recommendations. These people will be key players on your team, and you want to see how they fit into your plans.

You get to know your lenders. You meet with your company's banking-relationship managers and their superiors. You visit investment bankers who have had corporate projects with your company. You begin to understand their view of your assets and balance sheets.

You meet with account executives and outside service agencies—accountants, consultants, advertising agencies, public relations firms. You know what major projects are outstanding or contemplated. You get topflight people assigned to your company's account.

You review shareholder lists and seek out the important holders, individual and institutional. You appraise the investor-relations program and plans for annual and quarterly reports. You begin drafting your first letter to the shareholders.

You meet in cities around the country with the financial analysts who follow your industry. You meet with key

IMAGINE A CITATION THAT'S BEEN FLYING NONSTOP SINCE THE YEAR 1307.

That's how much flight time Citation business jets have logged. The fleet has accumulated an incredible six million hours of service.

It's the equivalent of one Citation flying night and day for 685 years.

It took more than just one to chalk up six million hours, of course. Nearly 2,000 Citations are now in service – the world's largest fleet.

So if you're looking for the business jet that more businesses fly, just look up. Chances are, there's a Citation passing overhead right now.

THE SENSIBLE CITATIONS

Cessna
A Textron Company

members of the press—particularly your industry's trade press. You learn your company's press policy or formulate one.

These activities are important, time-consuming, and detailed. Is it fair or logical to expect you to do all of these things so soon? Why don't you delegate most of this to your staff? How can you spend time doing this when so many high-priority decisions await your attention?

It does sound unfair to expect a new CEO to go through this corporate initiation at the expense of operating the company day to day. On the other hand, if a CEO doesn't learn about these activities in the first years of his reign, he may never catch up. What he learns now becomes the basis for his planning. So these are golden days, and the flurry of work that the Stage One CEO undertakes is exciting and useful.

Obviously these initial days aren't always golden. My own beginning, for instance, turned out differently. When recruiter Ward Howell convinced me to become CEO of the F. & M. Schaefer Corporation in July 1972, I told the company that I would begin on October 1, following a month's vacation in Europe.

But in late August, as I moved my books and papers to Schaefer, I saw that the current sales and profit information was alarming. The New York brewer had lost money in the previous year, come up with poor sales and another loss in the second quarter, and July sales slipped too. I told my wife we would not be going to Europe, that I was starting at Schaefer immediately.

Luckily she protested. So before heading for Europe, I asked my staff to have seven reports ready when I returned. These included a special cash forecast, a revised fourth-quarter estimate, a first cut at the following year's plan, a list of salable assets, and a closing plan for one of our four breweries.

It was a good strategy, because the staff could probably not have put the reports together while I looked over their shoulders. The reports were conclusive, and when I held my first board meeting on October 2, I declared a corporate crisis that remained in force my entire five years at Schaefer.

My problem became one of correcting difficulties while I

was still learning about the business, its people, and its stake-holders. I have ever since envied new CEOs who had the luxury of knowing their company and people better than I did before drawing up corporate and personnel plans.

Embracing the Board

For a new CEO of a publicly held company, the board of directors can be a vital ally in developing and executing company strategy. I have found this true not only as a CEO, but also as a director of a number of corporations.

In many cases you have been an outside director or are known to the board as a senior executive. In others you have come from outside the company or have not been intimately involved with the outside directors. Regardless, think of yourself as a newcomer, because your role as CEO is radically different from your former role as director or executive.

Good outside directors are a difficult lot. They are experienced and talented, often having had a full measure of CEO and board-chairman experience themselves. They have been elected to the board by the shareholders, frequently for three-year terms, feel secure in their posts, and are not necessarily subservient to the chief executive. You have had little to do with their selection, and they have a long-term working relationship with the retiring CEO, who may still be on the board. He may even still be chairman. It is a delicate situation to contend with as you try to win the directors over to your new ideas.

Those are good reasons to nurture your board when you are a Stage One CEO. After all, the directors hired you, and they can fire you. They determine your pay and that of your senior executives. They have to approve capital spending, financing moves, and major business plans. They monitor your performance, and they have great power. Be careful.

I can recall being impressed by a young Dwight C. Minton when, in his mid-thirties, he replaced his father as CEO at Church & Dwight Company, the makers of Arm & Hammer baking soda. As one of his outside directors, I had lunch with him every two or three months, and he would pepper me with questions: "What can we do to make our meetings more productive? Can you suggest changes to our agenda, our committee charters, our operating reports? Are you satisfied with the board material we send you?" He would talk about the impending activities of the company, saying that he could not afford to surprise any of the directors. And he always wound up our discussions by asking me to critique his dealings with the board and his actions as CEO.

Minton's behavior is a good model, but it is hard to duplicate. It requires security, it takes time, and not all directors are amenable to such an open approach. You may not be anxious to retain all of your inherited board members, which poses a delicate problem. You will need the support of your strongest directors to help you make a switch.

Organize a board that you can feel comfortable with, that will support you in times of crisis, and that will discuss issues candidly but not adversarially. And balance your board in age, talents, experience, knowledge, and influence. A board can get out of whack here, particularly under a long-term chairman, and it's a formidable task to reshape it.

In your first few months, your directors will give you a honeymoon. They are intrigued with your observations and the new directions you are thinking about. When the first one or two director openings occur, you'll have to convince those who remain that your nominees are the right caliber. If the directors feel you are packing the board too fast, your relationship can sour.

With the right membership and attitude, the board can be a powerful mentor. And the sooner you convince it to adopt your corporate and personal strategies, the better.

Building Your Team

As the incoming CEO, you will spend more time on personnel matters than on any other facet of governance. A CEO must have confidence in his management team, especially in those managers who report directly to him. If you have anticipated your selection as CEO, you will probably have decided on a tentative team by the time of your appointment. If you come from the outside, your first priority will be to appraise the direct reports you inherit.

1964

Board relations have been an area of emphasis for Dwight C. Minton (at right and with his father, Henry, the former chairman, above) since he became CEO of Church & Dwight in 1969.

◆

You must get to know all of the top people in some depth. You travel with them, eat and drink with them, meet their spouses, attend their meetings, analyze their performance, and have one-on-one sessions to discuss policies and programs. You ask for evaluations from informed observers in the human resources department, but also from customers, suppliers, bankers, accountants, directors, and retirees.

You assemble your team as soon as possible, stabilize it, and then test it for performance. Rare is the new chief executive who simply absorbs his predecessor's team. In fact, it is not uncommon to replace all or almost all of the direct reports. I had to at Schaefer; the team I inherited was just not able to move as rapidly or to change as much as I needed.

As you build your team, you are at your best. You are forced to think your program through so that your leaders can sell it to the organization. You count on them to weed out the underachievers, to cut costs, to lead the way to new products, new markets, new processes, and new standards. You may have to go to executive recruiters to find the expertise you need. And you have to oversee this time-consuming task personally because a wrong choice is very, very costly.

Now that a new CEO and some new senior executives are in place, you realign the company. You centralize or decentralize or eliminate levels of reporting. You consolidate or split up divisions and units. If the inherited structure has been in place for some time, you've got deadwood to prune. You may hire an outside consultant to speed up the process and to confirm your suspicions. Within a year of your appointment, you will have made significant organizational change and several major executive changes.

And while you're at it, you will invariably make processing and procedural changes. As you move through the company, managers will bombard you with ideas for improvement, and you are more receptive now than at any other time of your corporate life.

Today new CEOs are especially open to changes in computer use, communication systems, inventory strategies, statistical quality controls, personnel involvement programs, incentive compensation ideas, and other so-called modern management methods. You can spur an investigation of these new processes and their potential return.

You have covered a lot of ground. You have gotten to know your management people, heard what they think, held innumerable reviews of critical issues, and listened, listened, listened. (John Sculley, 53, CEO of Apple Computer, shows his title on his business card as "Chief Listener.")

Most of the quick and easy things have been started or done. You've removed simple roadblocks, cleared the bottlenecks, and slashed red tape. You have also cut cost where it hurts least.

For the most part, you have installed your own people in key spots. The company plans are now in your image and your name. The board has kicked off *your* annual profit plan, *your* capital project, *your* workout program, *your* incentive compensation system. It's your baby now.

People are getting used to your leadership. The board is content with its succession choice. It's time to blaze new trails.

If your company is typical, its long-range strategic plan was out of date when you took over. (Strategic plans, like new airplanes, are often obsolete by the time they leave the drawing board.) Many things have changed: legislation, foreign competition, the economy, technology. The old plan won't fly.

Now is your opportunity to solidify your vision for the company. That means you've got to translate your ideas into words and numbers that can be understood and implemented, outlining timetables, costs, and potential rewards.

To get a fresh start you go back to basics. You assemble your senior management team and head off for a weekend retreat. You hammer out a revised mission statement, review the company's strengths and weaknesses—as well as your competitors'—and plan alternate moves that can lead into fruitful areas. You hire consultants, appoint task forces, hold progress meetings. Finally, you present the plan to the board. It's adopted.

You now have a blueprint for your profit centers and a platform to share with employee groups. What you relate to financial analysts and shareholders and the press is now *your* vision of where the company is going.

Naturally, there are exceptions. Sometimes the new CEO inherits a well worked-out plan and may even have helped set it up. So change isn't warranted—and in fact may be dangerous. One young executive told me, "At my company, we've had three new CEOs in the last seven years. Each one felt he had to put in a new strategic plan. We have never been so screwed up."

But an approved strategic plan and a set of operating procedures are no more than expressions of desire. It is the follow-through that counts.

You begin to orchestrate the programs that will make your

plans come true. You lay out product-development schedules, implement marketing plans, hire consultants. To invest in new growth you pull the money from the company's cash cows or make widespread cuts. Since you are breaking new ground, you have to identify yourself with the projects; indeed, you must be their champion.

When you champion a product or project or person, you lose objectivity. You can no longer say, "I told you so," nor can you question the decision to go ahead. You and your project managers are locked in partnership, and you intend to make things work. One of the great qualities of CEOs in Stage One is that they are willing to take such risks to speed up the action and to get companywide enthusiasm.

This is a hard role, for often you have to play devil's advocate, questioning the merit of a future investment. But when you endorse a capital project or approve a new product or hire someone, you have committed yourself to the success of that project or person. Like a parent, you nurture and discipline.

As you look over your company, you will inevitably see product lines and segments of the business that no longer fit or produce. And you see gaps that have not been filled by traditional product- and market-development programs. You are in an excellent position to correct these situations, because you were not a party to creating them. Armed with your strategic-planning blueprint, you can move vigorously into the acquisition and spinoff arena.

In theory, spinoffs and acquisitions make sense. Sell off those businesses that do not fit and that produce inadequate returns; buy new businesses that fit and show promise of improved profits. This is harder to do than it sounds.

Good businesses that fit are not for sale, or they command absurdly high prices. Businesses you consider dogs, your potential purchasers view that way too. It takes time to review potential deals, do due diligence, and negotiate terms. If the deal falls through, you lose your time investment. Many acquisitions don't work out because they are mishandled as the acquiring company takes over. A new CEO is in a good position to supervise this transition; an older chief executive is more inclined to delegate this task.

Despite these problems, as a new CEO you will have the daring and tenacity to make changes in the business portfolio because the time is right for both you and the company.

Still, Murphy's law has never been repealed and never will be. Things will always go wrong and always at the worst of times. Newly hired and appointed executives won't work out, won't fit, won't get the job done as promised. Suppliers will deliver late or fall below your standards. Machines won't work and parts won't fit. Computers go down. Costs go up. Competitors cut prices. The Japanese bring out a new product. Your employees strike, and you sprain your ankle. You missed making profit plan, and that means you will not make the target bonus you set for yourself. Your key managers, who have worked so hard, will miss their target bonuses too. And next year doesn't look any brighter.

After you have been in office for two or three years, you look back and realize that you have had a productive time. Your vision of the company is increasingly clear, and the plan you have outlined is in place.

You have initiated scores of new programs. Total Quality Management is showing results. Lower-level people, even the unions, are coming up with cost-saving ideas. The new computer network is installed, although at higher cost than sketched. With fewer levels of management, communication is faster, time cycles are shorter, and more decisions are delegated. You have acquired a company, launched several products, and secured new global alliances.

So it goes. Work the glitches out. Reevaluate. Paint. Sweep. Clean up. Try again. And again. And again.

Have you completed your CEO task? No, dozens of things are left to do and to readjust—or, really, for the managers you have appointed to do.

Have you fulfilled the expectations of the people who elected you? Partially, but they don't fully appreciate how hard you've had to work.

Do you have the same old zip you possessed when you first tackled the job? Probably not. Why? You are about to enter Stage Two.

SENSIBLE BUSINESS DECISIONS GOT YOU WHERE YOU AR
THIS ONE TAKES YOU WHERE YOU WANT TO GO.

You've led your company through times in which others have failed. Thanks in no small part to your ability to act quickly and decisively.

But as the pace of the world quickens, you wonder if your company can continue to lead if it must follow airline schedules. For more than 1,500 businesses worldwide, the answer is no. They fly Citations.

It may surprise you to learn that a number of these companies are really not all that big. Yet.

THE SENSIBLE CITATIONS

Cessna
A Textron Company

Chapter Two

Stage Two: The CEO Discovers His Fellow CEOs

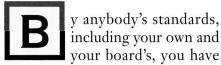y anybody's standards, including your own and your board's, you have been a hard-working, striving CEO. You have brought great vigor and positive change to the company. You have planned your work and worked your plan.

Something is missing. You aren't having as much fun.

Maybe it is too much travel. Too many meetings. Too many breakfasts and luncheons and dinners. Too much paper. Too many problems that drag on too long. Too many letdowns from people you counted on.

By now it is one more annual meeting, one more quarterly report, one more monthly board agenda, one more daily schedule. As Edwin Gee, former CEO of International Paper, told me, "My first catfish dinner at our Mississippi plant was great fun. My fifth was work." Is this the way it was meant to be?

What's missing is your anticipation of this inevitable tedium. The newness and excitement of Stage One crowded out any such idea. You have not planned for this next stage; in fact you had no formal personal plan at all.

So you're surprised as you lift your head from your daily priority list and look around. You see a scenario you barely noticed as you diligently pursued the job of a dedicated Stage One CEO.

You are about to discover your fellow CEOs.

As the CEO of a reasonably profitable, fairly sizable corporation, you are in the catbird seat to have the extracurricular time of your life.

You can afford it. You have a fine salary, bonus, pension plan, and the makings of a strong personal balance sheet. You have range and firepower. Your expense account takes you where the fun and games are. You can go first class and usually do.

Your staff handles tickets, reservations, correspondence, and phone calls. You often stay at a club, as a member or a guest, and miss the madding crowds. If you have a company plane, hooray!—you are in CEO hog heaven.

You can go where the action is. The Masters. The Super Bowl. The Kentucky Derby. The Indianapolis 500. The White House.

You mix with high-profile people. "Last week I sat next to Jack Nicklaus [or Tina Brown or Peter Jennings] at a dinner," you begin, "and I heard some very interesting things."

You cultivate a hobby. Salmon fishing. Opera. Quail hunting. Outward Bound.

But these are primarily amusements for your personal satisfaction. More important, you are now in position to plunge with your fellow CEOs into activities that are good for you and, with some justification, good for your company. And they are fun.

As chief executive, you are a prime candidate for an outside directorship of another corporation. You bring the recent experience of revamping your company, contributing ideas that save time and money. You comprehend and empathize with the problems and frustrations of a fellow CEO. You move in quickly as a peer; your credentials are easy to see. You are particularly useful as a member of the Organization and Compensation Committee because you understand how the systems work and, best of all, recognize the need for appropriate CEO compensation. In fact, you have such handsome qualifications that there simply aren't enough chief executives like you to go around as outside directors.

Of great pertinence is what you bring back to your company. You see how another CEO runs his meetings, uses his board committees, handles the agenda, and gets things done. As I certainly did, you learn a lot from the experiences of the 10 to 15 other directors participating in the board discussion. As you approve a shareholders' rights plan, your understanding of corporate governance increases. You begin building a resource network to keep from reinventing a lot of wheels.

Rawleigh Warner Jr., former CEO of Mobil Corporation, agreed. "A CEO is doing himself and his company a disservice if he doesn't take advantage of the opportunity to learn from other CEOs how to do his job more effectively," he told me. "A couple of befitting outside boards can teach him much at minimal time cost."

But which board invitations to accept? Make that decision part of your personal plan. You should, of course, avoid conflicts of interest and get along with the incumbent CEO. And look for companies that are about the same size or larger than yours, that have some cutting-edge technology, and that are highly regarded in their industry.

Politely refuse invitations from companies in financial trouble, in critical litigation, or in the midst of a fight or crisis. Few CEOs have the time to cope, and resigning from such a board can be embarrassing and time-consuming. Think twice about conglomerates also; as their director you may not serve on any other board whose company makes the same product. Your membership may also be a conflict as you and your company consider new acquisitions. And I dislike faraway boards: a nearby board meeting takes half a day; one 200 miles away might take two days.

"I advise CEOs to keep from making any decisions regarding outside activities for at least a year," said Thomas

J. Neff, president of Spencer Stuart, the executive search firm. "There is so much to do and to learn that they can't possibly judge what is best for them; as a matter of fact, the best invitations for boards and for other activities are usually not the first ones." Take a little time to think about it; talk to some members of your own board and to other chief executives.

Boards in a number of large cities, especially in the Midwest, are often replete with interlocking directorates. As a matter of local custom and pride, the top companies tend to add local CEOs to their boards; such invitations are difficult to decline. Major banks also seek the CEOs of their largest customers to be directors, and, as a result, a bank-board seat is prestigious.

Some companies offer undeniably attractive board invitations. A Fortune 100 company. An airline. A major sports or entertainment or publishing company. A company with an alluring location.

How to keep it all in bounds?

Robert E. Flynn, the 59-year-old CEO of NutraSweet in Deerfield, Illinois, has a stringent method for limiting the time he spends on outside activities. "I have five weeks of official vacation," said Flynn, also the former chief executive of Fisher Controls International, a process-control instrument manufacturer. "Three weeks of this I allot to serving on boards and participating in external affairs. I get the diversion I need, but I don't actually take the time away from my company."

Most CEOs aren't as tough on themselves as Flynn is, but if you are going on only two or three boards, plan carefully; choosing the right board can lead to a series of difficult choices. The invitations are an honor extended by important people. They offer the vista of long-term involvement at a high level, and these days they pay significant fees.

Part of business life in the United States is the network of industry trade associations—the Chemical Manufacturers Association, the American Petroleum Institute, the American Bankers Association, for example. These groups gather statistics, set industry standards, organize joint promotion and development, coordinate government relations, and discuss common problems. Their meetings provide about the only ethical opportunity to meet with the CEOs of your competitors and the CEOs of many related companies in your industry, which may also be present or potential suppliers, customers, licensees, and affiliates.

Can you avoid participating in trade-association activities? Probably not. It is an important part of your job, and you learn a lot from mingling. Someone from your company needs to participate in association affairs, and some of the time it should be you.

More optional but also more alluring are those great little meetings where CEOs get together to learn about critical issues or to discuss mutual problems. These get-togethers were, for me, one of the best things about being a CEO. I loved the reality check, finding out that other CEOs had just as many problems as I did, and sometimes more. I was delighted to come away with a new idea or approach that I could not possibly have dreamed up myself. And the meetings were a refreshing break from my demanding in-box and incessant telephone calls.

Some of these meetings are two- or three-day sessions sponsored by business schools or independent forum groups. Some are programs offered by continuing institutions such as the Conference Board, the Foreign Policy Association, and the National Association of Manufacturers.

Others are programs sponsored by invitational groups—like the Young Presidents Organization, the Management Policy Council, and the American Society of Corporate Executives—that meet at resorts to discuss mutual affairs and concerns. They often include spouses.

If you are invited to some of the meetings or to join one of the groups, consider accepting. Just remember that the time has to come out of something else.

Community programs are worthwhile as well. But there are so many, and they are all so needy. You may serve as co-chairman of the United Way drive or head up the Mayor's Development Committee or decide to join the church vestry.

EARLY IN HIS CAREER, MR. PALMER TURNED IN HIS CONVENTIONAL DRIVER FOR SOMETHING WITH CONSIDERABLY MORE LOFT.

Years ago, Arnold Palmer quit using automobiles for traveling to golf tournaments. For almost as long as we have built Citation business jets, Arnold Palmer has flown them.

Without the speed, convenience and reliability of Citations, Arnie says he couldn't possibly compete on the tour, design more than 100 golf courses, and manage his far-ranging business activities.

Mr. Palmer's game is golf, but his business is winning. So is his business jet.

THE SENSIBLE CITATIONS

Cessna
A Textron Company

The list is endless. And the sad truth is, the more you do and the better you are at it, the more you get asked to do.

Choosing a Backup

In your first year or two, you may hold all three of the top titles—chairman, president, and chief executive officer. This is not a bad situation if you have the vigor and the interest and the backing of the board. It is probably much too early for you to decide on a president and chief operating officer.

Now, as you add outside boards and activities and accomplish your programs, you should be ready to name a backup. It's a logical move: you are relatively secure in your job, and the board is beginning to press you on succession ideas. But be careful. Succession is one of the most delicate and thorny issues a CEO can face. There are several options:

You can appoint a seasoned executive as chief operating officer and make him president or executive vice-president. This will definitely reduce your workload, since the COO can travel the same routes you did, visiting facilities, meeting customers and suppliers, reviewing projects, and putting out fires. He may not be a long-term candidate for succession and so is not a threat. He is someone who can hold the fort if something happens to you and could continue as COO even under a new CEO. He may even be older than you. Whoever or whatever he is, he can surely make life better for a chief executive who has been functioning as both CEO and COO.

You can appoint a senior executive, such as the chief financial officer, to the post of vice-chairman. This is particularly appropriate when you don't enjoy the financial and administrative side of the business and are happy to delegate dealings with bankers, analysts, auditors, and shareholders. Again, he may not be a top candidate for succession and is no threat, but he makes it easier for an overloaded CEO to cope with his external activities.

You can appoint a bright, young, outgoing manager to be your backup and to represent you at a host of corporate affairs, somewhat as Bush did with Quayle. Over time he may or may not be able to work his way into position as your successor.

You may appoint the best person you can find, someone five to 10 years younger who has the potential to be CEO. However, many topflight managers won't take the COO job under those terms or, if they do, they are soon recruited to another company. For many CEOs anxious to continue their reign, it is too early to have an ambitious heir apparent pressing them. Anthony J.F. O'Reilly, 56, CEO of H.J. Heinz, recalled another chief executive's advice: "One of the most important things to remember as a new CEO is to identify your successor and then fire the bastard."

The COO's job is often hazardous, short-lived, and prey to a revolving door. But if you want to move sagely into Stage Two, you need a backup.

If you're like the CEOs I know, pay is important to you. The drive for a competitive salary is part of your psychological makeup. You are at the top of the pyramid and work under pressure. You have only a few years in office to make it big. So you want to be properly paid for good performance, for the responsibilities you shoulder and the risks you take.

Of course, what the retiring CEO made will inevitably affect what you make. The directors who approved his compensation package are still there and, often, so is the former CEO. You are untested in the post, and some question may remain about how you can handle certain facets of the job. You were given a big raise and a flock of options. You want the job. So you probably don't negotiate a special compensation deal at the start. (This is not true when a CEO is recruited from the outside.)

As the excitement of being CEO lessens and you ease into Stage Two, you begin to pay close attention to the annual salary revelations in *Business Week*, *Forbes*, and the financial newspapers. You become sensitive about where you stand in relation to CEOs from other companies in your industry and from companies comparable to yours in size and function. Invariably you find examples of CEOs doing better than you are in salary, bonus, and options. You *know* your job is more complicated, demanding, and critical than theirs. And, oh, the rub when you notice that some of your closest CEO friends have a better package than you do.

This is a crucial period in your CEO tenure. You are beyond the first trials, but before the specter of retirement. You have a track record and a set of goals. It is time to talk to the board about a long-term performance pay plan.

You have been a good CEO. If you are the CEO of a publicly held company, you have worked unceasingly to keep the board informed, to improve procedures, to listen to advice and counsel, to show them your ideas, your people, your programs. You run efficient meetings. You have put into effect many of the things you learned from being on outside boards. And outside directors enjoy serving on your board.

By now several of the older directors have retired, including your predecessor CEO. New and younger directors closer to your interests, attitude, and age replace them. In fact, they are often CEOs whom you have gotten to know through your new outside activities.

For the most part, a natural transition takes place as you gradually reorder the board. As a maturing CEO, you are becoming more a leader than a manager. You no longer require division heads to rehearse their board presentations with you. You let the CFO report more of the financial data. You bring fewer matters to the board in a problem stage and more matters that have already been acted upon; it is easier to ask for forgiveness than for permission. More and more of the board work is done in committee meetings, followed by routine board approval. You frequently call key directors before the board meeting to brief them on controversial matters, and they like that.

Overall you have put together a board that is good for the company—independent, participative, and supportive. Unless things go radically wrong, or unless you get too involved in outside activities, you are in charge.

You still visit company sites, but not as often as before; your new COO is doing more and more of that for you.

You fly frequently to the Greenbrier and the Homestead for trade-association meetings. To Palm Springs and Scottsdale for conferences. To a Young Presidents meeting in Puerto

IN 1995,
PEOPLE AROUND THE WORLD
WILL BEGIN DOING THE SIX-SECOND MILE.

You're looking at the fastest business jet in the world. At Mach .9, it does a mile in 6.06 seconds. And sprints LA-to-New York in under four hours.

It's the new Citation X. And it's the latest example of Cessna's commitment to the development of new technology. Our total investment in business aircraft research and support is now more than a billion dollars.

You can see for yourself the remarkable result of that investment when Citation X deliveries begin in 1995. But you'd better look fast.

THE SENSIBLE CITATIONS

Cessna
A Textron Company

Rico. To meet with your new European affiliates in Brussels.

You play golf and tennis with your fellow CEOs. You talk with them over lobster and beer. You hunt with them in the paper company forest lands. You get the inside story on Wall Street, the White House, Mike Milken, Bill Clinton, and Ross Perot. You go up the Hudson River on the Forbes boat and down the Colorado River with Ogilvy and Mather.

You're getting around.

As a Stage One CEO, you didn't use the executive dining room an awful lot. You were too busy traveling. Oh, you used it for lunch-time staff meetings when you were home, but mostly to save time.

Now that you are not on the road as much, you delight in having guests to lunch and occasionally to dinner. You always lunch there with your board committees and individual directors; you may even feel more comfortable there than in your office.

You get used to throwing luncheons for retiring executives, contest winners, or newly appointed managers. You have hosted the mayor, your congressman, your bankers, your stock specialist. You are quite gracious about entertaining company visitors from out of town—customers, suppliers, distributors—some of the people you used to see more regularly than you do now.

Best of all you enjoy having your fellow CEOs in for lunch from time to time—and going to their executive dining rooms with them. It is not always that grand. F. Kenneth Iverson, the 67-year-old CEO of Nucor Steel Corporation, famous for his no-frills approach, gleefully steers his guests across the street to his "executive dining room," a diner with Formica-topped tables.

As the long-term CEO of a company and as a distinguished, mature executive, you should expect and probably deserve a certain amount of high-class treatment and respect. On outside boards, you are now chairman of a major committee, an honor in board circles. That takes up a lot more time than serving as a committee member. Often you are on the executive committee or nominating committee as well.

You chair the boards of your favorite charities, but just

"for a year or two." At your trade association, your clubs, your discussion groups, you chair the annual dinner, the membership committee, the program for next year.

When things go awry at one of your outside boards—a tender offer, a management-succession crisis, a severe financial problem, major litigation—you're on the committee that gets into the details of the problem. The new young CEOs on the board don't have the time or the stature.

Where do *you* get the time to do these things? If they are a logical part of your overall plan, they should be no problem. But if you have not planned ahead, they may cut into time needed to manage the business.

Stop at Stage Two?

Life has changed since you were a first-stage CEO. Then you were full of your company, traveling constantly, dealing with affiliates, and scrambling to make your company more efficient, more productive, more profitable. You worked all the time.

Now you add a new dimension. Instead of using only the expertise of in-house managers and yourself, you have found a way to learn from talented and wise outsiders.

It is a heady experience. You have been quoted in *Business Week*, written up by Merrill Lynch, and honored at your college reunion. You're on a first-name basis with many of the CEOs featured in *Fortune*.

Have you become a better, more effective CEO? You think so. Your contributions are broader and more sophisticated. You are putting your management team to work and reviewing their performance. You share your expertise with colleagues who need and benefit from your attention.

It is time to review your personal plan and see where you are and where you want to go. Do so carefully; warning signals are flying all over the place that you could go beyond the point of no return.

It has been a few years since you moved into Stage Two. Your company is performing fairly well, moving along at the same pace as the industry, holding market share, and making an average return on investment. Your stock price is in line with the Standard & Poor's index, and you have exercisable options at hand. But is this a delusion of adequacy?

Your outside boards are still interesting, though more time-consuming than you wish. Last quarter you missed two outside board meetings.

At the same time, new kinds of competitors challenge your industry, and you are preparing an aggressive counter-promotion. You head up the hospital fund drive. You speak at the Distinguished Leaders Lecture Series at Columbia Business School. You host a meeting for the Management Policy Council.

You feel harried as your schedule overflows and your in-basket fills. Your trade magazines pile up. You turn down an invitation to play golf in the Hook 'n Eye tournament at Cypress Point. Your wife says you need a vacation.

These are early warning signals that you're heading into a classic challenge/choice situation. Should you clamp a curfew on outside activities and go back to being a full-time CEO? Should you reorganize the company or make a major acquisition? Should you rally everyone to try for the Total Quality Management Award? Should you get the company started in a new-growth area like biogenetics or fiber optics? What about forging a new set of global alliances?

Have you waited too long to do these things? Have you drifted too far along the daisy paths of Stage Two to go back to Stage One? Do you have the time, and would it disrupt your company if you did? Why had you not planned on this? I think you could have and should have realized this crossroads was coming.

So you ponder. You calculate how long it will be before mandatory retirement. (CEOs have trouble with this exercise.) You have less time than you thought. Have I reaped the fruits of my labor? you ask. Are there some things I should do before I give up my magic scepter? What are the most noble and global CEOs doing these days?

You are about to discover a new arena that you knew existed but had no time for and little interest in. You are about to discover the world beyond the corporate community.

Beware! This region, like Shangri-la, is filled with devilish time traps, exotic mazes, and endless vistas. If you know what you are getting into and plan your trip with care, you can have a wonderful passage. But if you have not prepared your company and yourself for Stage Three, you can easily get lost. This is the jumping-off place where CEOs separate themselves from reality and from their companies. As the old song says, "They don't come back, won't come back, once they're gone."

THE DAY A BUSINESS JET TAUGHT
THE SHISHMAREF FIRST-GRADE CLASS.

The Citation V's unique ability to fly long distances yet land on short airstrips has allowed it to get into some pretty remote places. One such place was the tiny, isolated town of Shishmaref, near the Arctic Circle.

When the Citation landed on a narrow snowplowed strip, children came running from the nearby school. They'd never seen a jet before.

And chances are, they may never see any others besides Citations. Unless Shishmaref builds a runway long enough for less versatile business jets to use.

THE SENSIBLE CITATIONS

Cessna
A Textron Company

Chapter Three

STAGE THREE: THE CEO DISCOVERS THE OUTSIDE WORLD

You have met your senator and are on a first-name basis with your governor. You and your wife attend the symphony ball and openings at the art museum. You are a dais sitter at charities, business school dinners, and Man of the Year ceremonies. Although you've had lots of opportunity to be more active, you've stayed aloof. You've simply been too busy running the company and coping with related CEO activities.

Now you're not so sure. It might be good for you and for the company to get involved in a few broader, more critical issues before you retire. What are *you* doing about the environment? About education? About corporate governance? About free enterprise? You want to make a more noticeable contribution to society.

This phase starts when another CEO asks you to serve on a committee in Washington, D.C. You find it exhilarating. You are impressed by the knowledge and dedication of top government officials. The problems you discuss are of great importance to the country and of surprising interest. You and several other CEOs form a subcommittee and meet again.

You enjoy going to Washington and learning your way around. This is where the action is. The President's Advisory Committee for Trade Policy and Negotiations. The Republican (or Democratic) Party Committee. The Council for Citizens Against Government Waste.

It wasn't all that difficult to join the Business Council and to meet other CEOs, not only in Washington, but also in your local chapter. You loved those programs at the Homestead in Hot Springs; you hope someday to become a vice-chairman in charge of one of next year's programs. It feels pretty good to be right there with the government's economic advisers.

Who knows, you may even get lucky enough—or your company big enough—for you to be one of the 200 members of the *crème de la crème* Business Roundtable. And if you get named to the 44-man policy committee, well, that's about as far as a country-boy CEO can go.

You mingle with interesting people. You get to know senior staffers at the Department of Commerce and bureaus and agencies related to your industry. You meet lobbyists and the trade-association representatives who grind axes for you.

You begin to dabble in fund-raising and co-chair as many dinners and luncheons as you have time and money for. And once you're ensnared in national politics, you're fair game for state and local action as well. You simply have more status in Denver, Dover, or Des Moines if you've played the Washington course.

Altogether, the exposure is fascinating, flatters your ego, expands your base, and gives you new things to talk about with friends. Few events offer greater bragging rights than dinner at the White House. (This I know. My wife and I were invited when President and Mrs. Reagan hosted a dinner for the Danish ambassador. We got all dolled up and were dazzled to meet Danny Kaye, Dan Rather, and Donald Regan, among others. We found ways to drop it into the conversation for months.)

But you don't need to go to D.C. Every city has prestigious organizations whose boards offer coveted directorships.

You can mingle with old money, new money, and household names—and if your company acts as benefactor, the cost is low. If you can't or don't want to play in these circles, hundreds of less publicized but equally alluring organizations would love to add a well-connected CEO to their boards.

Similarly, every city has national and local social service groups that need money and help: the American Cancer Society, Planned Parenthood, United Negro College Fund. Each has at least one CEO on its board whose mission is to get more CEOs and companies interested and involved. Serving as a director of a well-endowed foundation is also compelling.

But sometimes the pressure to engage in outside activities affects your work. Robert A. Burnett, 65, told me that when he became CEO of Meredith Corporation, the large publishing firm in Des Moines, his office was inundated with requests for sponsorship. "I was drowning in good deeds," said Burnett. He hired a manager of community relations, established a contributions committee, and decided on a set of classified priorities for himself. Only then was he able to open the valve and take on some outside action.

Frequently these outside activities create an unusual retirement opportunity. After 10 years as CEO of Lever Brothers, the consumer package goods company, Thomas S. Carroll began planning for retirement. He called business schools for ideas and let each of his outside boards know his plans. When he retired three years later, he offered to resign from all his directorships, including one with the International Executive Service Corps. Frank Pace Jr., then its chairman, responded instead by asking Carroll to succeed him. Over 12 years that position has taken Carroll all over the world. "The perfect way for a CEO to keep from going too far into Stage Three," said Carroll, 73, "is to retire early and start a whole new career."

Was Carroll lucky? Perhaps, but he created his luck by having a variety of outside relationships, by seeking information from his peers and from business schools, and by developing a plan.

Nearly all CEOs these days are college graduates, and

an increasing number hold graduate degrees. Many have a continuing interest in their old schools, and their schools definitely have a continuing interest in them. It all starts so simply. You are asked to give a talk at the University of Colorado Business School or Georgia Tech. You do a three-day executive-in-residence bit at Dartmouth. You receive the outstanding alumnus trophy at Ohio Wesleyan. You join the Stanford Business School Advisory Council.

Naturally the schools expect money from you and your company, and they want you to raise money by impressing others with your solicitation. And they especially want you and your company to be involved in the school's academic research.

CEOs who were not particularly good scholars are often intrigued with academic research. Their company may endow a strategic study research project or set up an international institute for the privatization of Hungarian industry. They may invite Harvard Business School into their company to write one of those famous HBS cases. Or they may sponsor a series of lectures and establish an endowed professorship or scholarship fund in their name or their company's name.

Giving money to your former school and seeing it invested the way you want can be a rewarding experience. Jerome A. Chazen, CEO of Liz Claiborne and a member of the Columbia Business School's Board of Overseers, has a longstanding interest in education and a global approach to business. Last year he gave a $10 million gift to establish the Jerome Chazen Institute of International Business at the business school.

"We can now move forward to shape a new international, interdisciplinary vision of business management education," said Meyer Feldberg, dean of Columbia Business School. "This is an integral part of Jerry Chazen's personal plan and a wonderful way for a successful CEO to make a positive and lasting contribution."

Renewing the old school tie need not be confined to academics. Some CEOs delight in acting as benefactors to the Boosters Club, their fraternity, or good old Skull and Bones. Joel E. Smilow, the 59-year-old CEO of Playtex, endowed a chair for the head football coach at Yale. The link may not even be to your old school. As a Woodrow Wilson fellow for several years, I lectured at small colleges around the country and found it great conversational fodder.

Do all these activities take time? Of course. A CEO in Stage One is too immersed in his company; a CEO in Stage Two is too busy running around. As a CEO in Stage Three, you feel much freer to join in. After all, these organizations need your experience and help, you have given years of time to your company, and you rather like the limelight.

Nothing is wrong with adopting a Stage Three stance, and making a meaningful contribution feels great. To an extent, you owe it to yourself and to society. And properly handled, it can be valuable to you and your company; it adds to your contacts and enhances the company's image. The danger is that you can go in too soon, stay too long, and get in too deep. That, of course, is why you need a plan.

Some of the best CEOs I have ever observed were able to contribute simultaneously to business and society. They did excellent work in Washington, were a force in their communities and in their charity work. But a chief executive too wrapped up in ancillary games can become a partial CEO. He clings to his power even as he becomes almost dysfunctional in terms of current knowledge and information. It could happen to you.

When you first became a CEO, you were invited to sit on the dais at a few affairs and occasionally did so. You didn't find it particularly exciting, didn't know many of the luminaries, and found the speeches trite. Now, however, as a long-term CEO and prominent citizen, you are sought to anchor the dais for all kinds of affairs. And you are obligated to repay the dinner chairman or the guest of honor whom you badgered to sit on your dais earlier: "I will sit on the dais at the University of Chicago annual dinner if you will do it for me at the Northwestern banquet." Or "When you were honored by B'nai B'rith, I took a table and sat on the dais; now it's your turn." The circle is insidious.

As a polished speaker with a recognizable name, you may introduce Henry Kissinger at a Woman's Club luncheon, present the guest speaker at the Wharton School of Business dinner, and receive a few plaques yourself as, if nothing else, a consistent donor of company tables.

You get to be proficient at dais sitting. You don't get trapped in the back row or off to the side. You meet the right people, chat with the prime honorees, and see that you are seen. One CEO contended this was one of his most important activities: his dais sitting placed his company in the limelight. That's going too far.

Of course, you don't confine your CEO work to the outside world. You love showing up at the company retirement dinners, giving talks, and handing out 25-year pins and watches. You rise to the occasion, at your best as you praise old friends. This lets everybody know that you are still there, still smart and tough, and still to be reckoned with despite the distractions of the outside world.

When a CEO starts exploring that world, he discovers new roads and treasures. You can go to the Aspen Institute, the Japan Society, or a variety of think tanks to discuss heady questions with learned people. You can take courses on the Great Books or go to scintillating lectures on profound subjects.

You travel compulsively, heading out to Singapore for a *Business Week* conference with Southeast Asian CEOs or to Moscow with a Yale alumni tour. If you have a special interest in any country or region, you can find a related group that wants active, way-paying CEOs to join in.

Once you begin to taste the international life, you can't get enough. During Stage One and Stage Two, you were primarily concerned with the domestic aspects of your business. But through your contacts with other companies and outside sources, you now realize that you have neglected a whole new arena.

It doesn't take long to start worrying about your company's posture in the European Community or its role on the Pacific Rim or its standing in Latin America. Your trips to Budapest and Hong Kong and Sao Paulo are wondrous adventures. And your interest in Japanese competition, Russian privatization, and free trade with Mexico rises.

Interestingly enough, you could be right. Your company has neglected its global affairs, and that was partially your fault—though lots of American companies have been late in formalizing a global posture. You may be making a useful contribution, especially if you synchronize your personal plan with your corporate plan.

Letting Your Job Slip Away

As you spend more and more time away from the workaday routine, you get the illusion that you are a member of a favored, even royal, class. You have forgotten how to stand in line, how to take public transportation, how to dial the telephone. When you go to an event, you sit in the owner's box, eat in the "club" dining room, and go backstage after the show.

You travel to special enclaves such as "the Grove" in California. You attend special dinners with the Alfalfa Club. You belong to the U.S. Seniors and play golf with the old boys at Lyford Cay and Mountain Lake and Maidstone.

You cling to all your old toys, but it's not the same. You take the company plane and limo for more personal trips (to the dismay of your controller) and carry more friends as passengers. You use the company apartment more often for cocktail parties than for business meetings.

You still keep a high profile because you love to hear the applause and the roar of the crowd. But you like to pick the places and the crowds.

The danger in Stage Three is that you may be running away from reality. You are bored by the routine of managing the company, by the drawn-out process of improvement, and by the frustration of setbacks. You found new excitement in Stage Two with your fellow CEOs, but now that too has begun to pale. As you explore the noncorporate world, you run into a familiar dilemma: being a CEO is just not as exciting as it was in Stage One or Two.

Once again you ask yourself, *Why not go back and start running the company all over again?* The answer is obvious. You are out of practice, and events have passed you by. New people are running new programs that you barely know about.

The projects you once championed have gone sour or been absorbed into the company's mainstream.

Instead of retaking command, you go in the opposite direction. You spend more time at your country hideaway and retreat off-season to the Hilton Head condominium you bought for retirement. To your chagrin, no one tries to find you.

When you come into the office, you tie yourself up with luncheon dates, outside boards, charity meetings, and personal affairs; it becomes difficult to see you.

You lunch every day with the same old cronies at the same old table at the same old club. You hear no new ideas, no conflicting opinions, no young voices. You push all of the difficult and dirty decisions down to the COO. When you disagree with decisions, you get churlish. You complain about the COO to your board, and sometimes, in near William S. Paley fashion, you get rid of him. This precipitates a managerial crisis, which catapults you back into action. You are more a nuisance than a help.

During this retreat from actively managing the business, it's not uncommon for CEOs to change a few other things. Their lifestyle. Their manner of dress. Sometimes their wives. They also change their perspective, almost losing sight of the pragmatic aspects of making a profit and keeping the business going.

This does not happen to all CEOs, of course. For many CEOs, Stage Three is the most enjoyable part of their career. They keep in touch; they know what they are doing and where they are going; they keep their balance.

In essence the CEO who loses his balance in Stage Three retires on the job. He forces the company to pay him for not working, even for causing problems. Everybody is cheated, including the shareholders.

It is fair to ask why a CEO is allowed to retire on the job. What can be done to prevent it? Whose responsibility is it, anyway?

THE U.S. LEADER
ELECTED BY THE ENTIRE WORLD.

Of all the business jet choices today, one line is the undisputed leader. One is chosen by more companies than any other.

Before choosing, most companies carefully evaluated several candidates. They looked at overall performance and operating cost. They compared safety records. Reliability. Cabin comfort. And support networks.

Then companies in 49 U.S. states and in 58 other nations all arrived at the same sensible conclusion. They all bought Cessna Citations.

THE SENSIBLE CITATIONS

Cessna
A Textron Company

Chapter Four

DEVELOPING
A PERSONAL PLAN

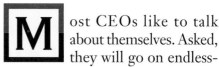ost CEOs like to talk about themselves. Asked, they will go on endlessly about their management style, their philosophy of leadership, and the character traits important to CEO success. They have no qualms about describing vital influences or business decisions that led them to the top. They have almost total recall for anecdotes, people, and places.

When it comes to discussing their personal agenda, however, CEOs are curiously reluctant to get into details. Why?

CEOs consider their personal plans private. Their plans may involve ideas and schedules for achieving power, prestige, position, or money that they are loath to admit. They may include negative elements such as bypassing or removing a senior director or former CEO who is acting as a roadblock.

Much of a CEO's life is an open book—his salary, stock holdings, incentive plans, pension arrangements, and perquisites may all be published in public proxy statements. His business decisions and forecasts are documented for his board and shareholders to critique. As a high-profile person in the business community, he knows even his private affairs are newsworthy. Is it any wonder that he shies away from talking with outsiders about his personal aspirations?

A CEO's personal plans are subject to constant and rapid change. An agenda is hard to pin down. The neophyte has so many new things to dig into, so many unfamiliar influences, that he says, "Why plan today when so much hinges on my meetings next week, next month, next year?" Few things in a CEO's life are easier to postpone than a personal plan.

Many CEOs want to "succeed" before they make personal plans. Over and over, CEOs told me, in effect, "The all-important element in my life right now is to make the company go. I have a flock of stock options and performance shares that can pay out big over the next few years. If and when they do, then I'll sit down and plan my way through the stages. Until then, I'm sticking to my knitting."

A CEO's personal goals tend to be fuzzy. The annual profit plan, the long-range strategic plan, the critical tasks of a chief executive are quantified and measurable. Not his personal plan. "I may someday want to do such and such," he says about his agenda, "but it depends on such and such."

Many CEOs are insecure about their tenure. Once upon a time, when a CEO was elected, he could count on keeping his post until he retired or died. Not anymore. Several hundred CEOs lose their jobs each year through acquisitions, leveraged buyouts, or bankruptcy. Others, with increasing frequency, are forced out by their boards after poor corporate or personal performance. Few CEOs are willing to admit to a feeling of inadequacy or insecurity, but such feelings do influence their long-term planning.

When I pressed my CEO friends to admit that they *must* have thought about matters such as outside boards, community affairs, the timing for succession, and their involvement in extracurricular activities, they responded, "Oh, sure. I do some of that. But I never sat down and wrote out what I would describe as a strategic plan, nor do I have a formal schedule that I execute in an orderly, comprehensive way."

In my opinion CEOs *are* thoughtful about personal planning. Many of them think about it all the time. But the peculiar circumstances of their job and their company tend to keep them from formalizing a plan until they near retirement. Let me give you a few examples.

John J. Burns Jr., CEO of the Alleghany Corporation, a financial services company in New York City, told me, "I guess I should be ashamed to tell you that I have never really had a personal plan—and here I am, president of this big company for 15 years. Most of my excuse is that I identify myself so closely with the company. I may be one of those characters who are thought to no longer exist—a 'company man.'"

Burns has tried to look ahead in five-year segments not unlike the three stages. "Now that I'm 61, I am beginning to plan things more tangibly," added Burns. "How long do I want to continue working, how do we want to organize our five businesses, what kind of management structure should we end up with? This is personal planning, but it is part and parcel of our corporate planning."

Robert Flynn, the disciplined CEO of NutraSweet, is so closely tied to the fast-changing situation of his company that his professional agenda governs his personal plans.

"I keep what I call a general sheet," said Flynn. "This is not much more than a calendar which helps me coordinate my incessant international travel program and my personal life. I don't extend this calendar beyond two or three years; that's as far out as I can see."

Still, at 59, Flynn is anxious to clarify his next six years of work. He plans to continue his interest in juvenile diabetes after retirement though his original involvement stems from NutraSweet. And he's bought a house in Palm Beach, where he'll do more and more of his work.

A CEO has to correlate his personal with his corporate planning. Peter C. Meinig, CEO of HM International, a diversified manufacturing organization in Tulsa, initially had no other plan than to work hard, take risks, and survive. But now that he has three businesses under way, he plans to have three executives run each of those companies.

"Although I expect to work forever," said Meinig, 53, "I am now able to think about allocating my time between my

Robert E. Flynn addresses a Juvenile Diabetes Foundation benefit in Hawthorn Woods, Illinois. Though his interest in diabetes is a natural outgrowth of his work as chief executive of NutraSweet, Flynn plans to continue his involvement after retirement.

◆

company, my family, my outside activities in Tulsa, skiing, and travel. I think it's a damned good plan. I just need to set a schedule and try to hold to it."

I also asked James A. Curtis, the CEO of Milliman & Robertson, an actuarial consulting firm in Seattle, about his personal planning approach.

"When my predecessor turned over the job to me 10 years ago," said Curtis, 65, "he told me that my top personal priority was to develop my replacement. I never forgot it. He has now been chosen, and I am moving up to chairman for a year before I retire."

Although Curtis always tried to think ahead, he never put anything into writing. Every once in a while he'd say to himself, "Curtis, you gotta get organized."

"I hate to admit being so typical," said Curtis, "but the

three stages are exactly what I went through. I had the same feelings and concerns about keeping in balance. Looking ahead helped, but the best thing I did was to keep in close touch with my board."

Cyril C. Baldwin Jr., CEO and chairman of Cambrex Corporation, a specialty chemicals company in New Jersey, has had to plan his way within the confines of a leveraged buyout. "When you commit yourself to a leveraged buyout, as my partner and I did 10 years ago," says Baldwin, "and then keep on buying companies and arranging new financing, your personal plan can get overwhelmed by your rapidly changing corporate situation."

Despite his workload, however, Baldwin has arranged for his succession, adjusted his schedule so that he can concentrate on acquisitions and international growth, and managed to participate in a few outside activities.

"I plan to retire in two years," said Baldwin, 65, "and I think that both the company and I will be in good shape. But I don't think I have ever moved all the way out of Stage One."

The CEO of a turnaround situation has special pressures of his own. John O. Whitney, 64, now teaching at Columbia Business School, talked about his experiences as president of Pathmark, a division of Supermarkets General: "The most compelling element of the turnaround CEO's job is survival. Almost every waking hour must be spent in finding cash, cutting expenses, saving customers, and pacifying creditors. His Stage Two comes when he gets his first positive cash flow and can take Sundays off. His Stage Three comes when he goes into the black, restructures his debt, and occasionally has a weekend free. Then, for the first time, he has a chance to start preparing a personal plan."

When you have a short reign as chief executive, you face a short personal planning cycle. My own case is a good example. When I accepted the CEO post at F. & M. Schaefer, I agreed to only a five-year tenure, knowing that I wanted to retire early and teach at a graduate business school. I also asked Schaefer to allow me to go on some outside boards, since I was virtually pensionless. I immersed myself in work for a couple of years and ultimately joined four New York

SHORTLY AFTER FLYING IN A CITATION, HUNDREDS OF PASSENGERS HAVE GONE ON TO BECOME CELEBRATED SPORTS HEROES.

In 1987 and again in 1991, hundreds of Citation owners volunteered their aircraft, pilots and fuel to airlift thousands of athletes to the International Special Olympics Games. The airlift was organized by Cessna. But the generous cooperation of Citation owners brought it to reality.

When we asked Citation owners to help these special people celebrate life in an unforgettable way, they didn't think twice.

They did it twice.

THE SENSIBLE CITATIONS

Cessna
A Textron Company

City boards. In my last year I went on the Dean's Advisory Board at Columbia Business School, prior to becoming executive-in-residence. I didn't recognize the stages then, but I telescoped all three into a five-year period.

Robert S. "Shell" Evans, 48, became CEO of Crane Company at 40 and, as such, had 25 years to look ahead before retirement, far more than most CEOs. During most of the eight years, he has acted as chairman, president, and CEO of the diversified manufacturing company—and as chairman and CEO of Medusa Corporation, spun off in 1988.

Despite plans to join outside boards, he has been so busy organizing and managing the companies that he has consciously refrained from getting into other activities. "Do I think I will ever get so overcommitted to outside activities that Crane will suffer?" asked Evans. "I doubt it. My work is much more interesting than anything else I do, and it is going to be several years before I know what Crane is going to be like. Until I do, my agenda is pretty full."

Another young man, Robert W. Mendenhall, is president and CEO of Wicat Systems, a small computerized learning systems company in Orem, Utah, acquired by Jostens Learning Corporation in August 1992. At 38, he has been CEO for five years and has been with the company all of his working life. After a board meeting, I cornered him about his personal planning program. He told me he keeps a journal of company changes, predictions, and ideas about how to respond.

"Every year I set out my personal goals, somewhat like making New Year's resolutions. Some of these goals have little to do with my company. I may promise myself to lose weight or improve my tennis or read more to my children."

A number of his personal goals, however, do relate to work. For instance, he plans to cut a 60-hour week to 55 and spend the extra five hours on outside activities.

"Mostly I plan a year or so ahead; sometimes I'll go three or four years out. But I can't quite call it a plan. My overriding goal is to make my company so successful that I will be in a position to do something else. My plan changes all the time, but that's what being a CEO is all about."

Some chief executives developed a personal planning approach for themselves long before they became CEO. Tom R. Horton, the former CEO of the American Management Association, explains in his new book, *The CEO Paradox*, the planning approach he worked out as an executive at IBM. First he listed his age in five-year intervals starting with age 5 and then labeled three columns: Strains, Goals, and Accomplishments. At each five-year mark, he wrote down what had concerned him then, what he had hoped would happen in the future, and finally what he had accomplished.

"Then I took the plunge," said Horton, "asking myself what I wanted to accomplish during the next five years, including precisely how I'd change the situation I was in. I've stuck with this system and recently filled out the chart for age 65. Looking back at 60 years of strains and gains has been illuminating."

The hardest part of personal planning for CEOs is getting started. As you can see from the prior examples, there's no set format, no printed form to fill in, no school to go to. The answer is in the advertisement for Nike athletic shoes, "Just do it!" Here are some suggestions that might help you get going:

Do it now. The time to make out your first personal plan is as close to your first day in office as you can handle. If you have known (or suspected) for some time that you will be named CEO, you are in an ideal position to set up a personal plan as you prepare for office. If you are recruited or if the appointment comes unexpectedly, then you'll need to wait a few months until you see the lay of the land. Whenever I moved to a new company or a new job, I found that around three months later I had the clearest vision; I knew enough about the business to think ahead, but not the reasons I wouldn't be able to act.

If you can't do it now, decide when you will. I like January 1. I frequently have free time over the Christmas holidays; this coincides with the start of annual planning at most companies; the newspapers are full of reviews and forecasts; and, of course, it's time for New Year's resolutions. You might prefer the anniversary of your appointment as CEO, your birthday, or the day of your annual physical examination.

Keep it simple. A yellow pad and pencil are fine. So are work sheets with columns. And two or three pages ought to be plenty.

Split your plan into several sections:

• The corporate life. List things you want to do that relate closely to your work life: organizational thoughts, board makeup, management communication, time allocation. Be as specific as you can about timing and dates.

• Outside activities. List those you want to get involved with: boards, trade association, community affairs, charitable programs, clubs. Again, be specific about time-frames.

• Retirement thoughts. Include a preliminary guess about when you will retire, management succession, special projects, and activities you want to continue after retirement.

Notice that these three sections coincide almost exactly with a CEO's three stages.

Do it annually. The world changes rapidly and so do CEO lives and thoughts. So rethink your personal plan at least once a year. When you do, start from scratch. Don't reread last year's plan until you have a new one. You'll be surprised at how much your thinking has changed. And don't be afraid to break into your planning process when a major event has occurred, such as a large acquisition. If and when your corporate perspective changes, your personal outlook will probably shift too. Go back to your plan.

Keep a file. Make one file folder for your annual personal plans. Keep another where you can drop clippings and notes reminding you of potential changes and additions to your plan.

Decide when to talk with someone else about your plan. Your personal plan is private. However, there will be times when it is useful to discuss your plan with a mentor, your wife, a member of your board, another CEO, or a consultant.

Unto thine own self be true. You don't need to hide anything in a personal plan. Face up to reality. Recognize your obstacles and plan how and when to overcome or neutralize them. Set sensible goals and schedules. Don't be shy about planning for greater job satisfaction and happiness. And don't leave out important ambitions because you don't yet know how to handle them.

When you take the time to develop a personal plan and then make a sincere effort to keep it current and realistic, you give yourself better odds of avoiding a bad mistake early in your career. Too many CEOs outline goals and decide on extracurricular activities without the benefit of a long-term plan. They look for the best opportunity as propositions are made and delay thinking about where they lead.

The future cannot be predicted. Because of this, and not in spite of this, CEOs need to see where they are heading. You do know that you will have a period of concentrated work, that you will be asked to participate in a number of outside activities, and that someday you will retire. So it behooves you to be as prepared as possible.

THE MEN WHO MANAGE CESSNA AIRCRAFT COMPANY HAVE HAD ONE THING IN COMMON EVER SINCE THEY WERE BOYS.

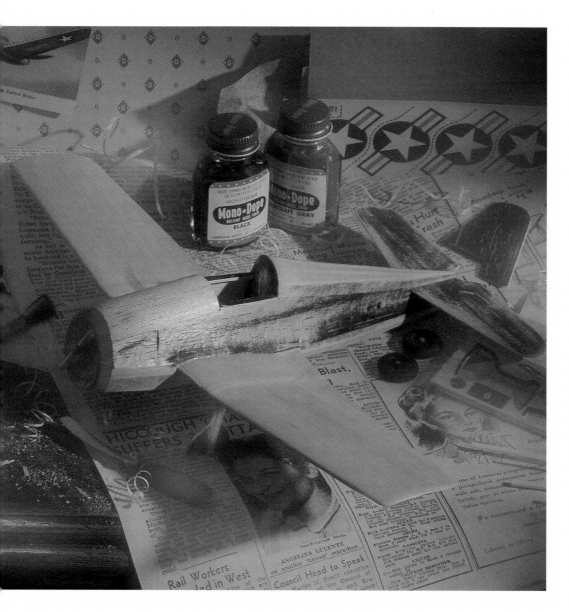

You could call it a lifelong fascination with aviation. You might even call it an obsession. Whatever it is, Cessna's top executives have never outgrown it. All of them are active pilots.

Some would say you don't have to be a pilot to build a good airplane. And they're probably right. But to build a great airplane, we believe it takes something beyond mere aerodynamics and aluminum.

We believe it takes a little passion.

THE SENSIBLE CITATIONS

Cessna
A Textron Company

Chapter Five

KEEPING YOUR BALANCE

hy is it that the personal and corporate lives of many CEOs get out of balance? All kinds of lower-level executives and professionals manage extracurricular activities as well as basic jobs. Why are CEOs different? I suspect there are three prime reasons:

The nature of the man and the job. CEOs are competitive. Frank T. Cary, asked how he got to be CEO of IBM in 1973, said, "I was at the right place at the right time because I went to work for IBM when it had only $200 million in sales. But I had to compete 21 times for jobs, and I won every time."

All the way to the top, CEOs have had goals to reach and competition to get there. Once the big goal is attained, it's hard to get out of the habit of accepting challenges and winning. For some CEOs, running a complicated, dynamic business is enough. But others have an insatiable need for new conquests.

A CEO on the way up has always had bosses to counsel him and to serve as mentors. When he becomes CEO, the loneliness of leadership sets in quickly. The new CEO determines his own pace, picks his own parameters, and defines his own limits. Sometimes he miscalculates.

Two top CEO recruiters, Thomas Neff of Spencer Stuart and J. William Stack Jr. of William Stack Associates, cited another important factor. Almost without exception, they agreed, no newly appointed CEO is fully prepared for the job. He may have had superb experience as the president of a General Electric operating division or as a global marketing executive for IBM or even as the president, COO, and inside director of a company in the same industry. But it is not the same. A new CEO has a full docket of things to learn about. While he can be very aggressive on the operating side of the business, he is often insecure about planning his extra-curricular activities.

The impact of power. A new CEO is surprised by his sudden power. When he barks, people jump. He can control the lives of people who work for him or who sell products and services to his company. Most of the time, no one tells him what he can or cannot do. Using his power to further personal interests and desires—sometimes to an absurd degree—can be an easy transition.

When a CEO is able to dominate his company—either through ownership, board cronyism, or sheer personality—he is most susceptible to misusing his power. He tends to overcompensate himself, flaunt his perquisites, and stay in office too long.

Pressure from others. As if the new CEO's own pressure to succeed isn't enough, a flock of other pressure points appear.

His people, especially his management group, have literally thousands of things for him to do. The shareholders, the lenders, the financial analysts all want early positive results. His board expects clear-cut management decisions and no mistakes.

His calendar and mail bulge with invitations to speak, to meet, to travel, to join, to chair, to listen, to give, to share. These appeals come from powerful, persuasive, persistent people. It frequently seems easier to give in than to resist.

His well-meaning fellow CEOs apply the most potent

pressure. Their siren call is to get away from the unrelenting humdrum office duties. "Come sit on my board, go to my seminar, meet my senator, join my club." And, toughest of all, "I did it for you; you do it for me."

Few CEOs can escape the velvet trap of overbooking before they learn to resist. Some learn before irretrievable excess. Some never learn.

I have thought a lot about what chief executives must do to stay in balance as they go through the three stages. A personal plan helps to narrow outside activities, prevent overbooking, and establish priorities. A good plan badly handled, however, can produce dismal results. So what can we learn from successful CEOs? What special approaches do they take to their jobs? How do they execute both a corporate and a personal plan?

Let me mention three factors common to well-balanced CEOs and then offer a few examples.

Enjoyment. Most chief executives I know enjoy being CEOs. And job enjoyment often accompanies job effectiveness. Like Dennis Weatherstone, the 61-year-old CEO of J.P. Morgan & Company, arguably the best bank in the United States, many prospering CEOs can say, "I enjoy going to work every day."

Listen to Dean Feldberg of Columbia Business School: "A successful CEO has to be excited and enthusiastic about his job, his company, and his constituencies. When the job becomes mundane, it is time to get out."

James W. Kinnear III, 64, CEO of Texaco, who has had more than his share of crises, said of his life and work, "To know what other people are thinking is one of my ongoing pleasures."

Vision. The ability to express what a company's future can and should be—and to do so with enthusiastic endorsement—is another quality of a successful and well-balanced CEO. Unless you can see what lies ahead, setting up and executing a personal plan is difficult.

Over the last seven years, I have served on the panel of CEO judges who choose the Chief Executive of the Year for *Chief Executive* magazine. As we reviewed the nominees' track records, we found that the quantitative measures were fairly apparent; the qualitative ones were more elusive. Inevitably, our discussion led to an appraisal of not only what the CEO had contributed to his company, but also how he compared to his fellow CEOs, and how he participated in company-related activities.

The crucial question nearly always boiled down to, "Which nominee has most sensibly enunciated a vision of his company's role and strategy and then done something about it?"

Glance at a partial list of our award-winning CEOs— Charles F. Knight of Emerson Electric, D. Wayne Calloway of PepsiCo, J. Willard Marriott Jr. of Marriott Corporation, Anthony J. F. O'Reilly of H. J. Heinz, Donald E. Petersen of Ford. All of these CEOs articulated a brave new vision for their companies and then worked unceasingly to realize it.

Staying power. Holding on to your job requires staying power. As we have seen, many CEOs cannot sustain their drive as they move through the three stages without neglecting their basic business. Yet some have been able to do it all.

I have referred to Dwight Minton, CEO of Church & Dwight. Not yet 60, he has been CEO for almost 25 years. When he took over from his father, his company had less than $20 million in sales; now it has $500 million, virtually all of which has come from internal growth. As his company grew, Minton made three complete changes in his direct reports. He knew how to adapt his people, his technologies, and his strategies as his company matured.

Among other CEOs I have known over the last 30 years, three stand out for their ability to maintain their balance and their staying power. As individuals, they are radically different in personality, managerial style, education, and work experience, and in the corporate environment they've developed.

Rawleigh Warner Jr., former CEO, Mobil Corporation. I met Rawleigh Warner in the late '60s. We both lived in Connecticut and commuted to New York City on the New Canaan Car, a private railroad car for business executives. The car seats faced inward, a good arrangement for conversation.

Warner participated vigorously in these daily discussions about the "news behind the news" in *The New York Times* and *The Wall Street Journal*. I was amazed at how many people and companies he knew and how much he had picked up about the business world.

At that time, Warner was 48 years old and had just become CEO of Mobil, so I have watched him operate for 25 years. The job fit him like a glove. He had good connections in the oil industry, got on the fast track early at Mobil, and didn't slow down after he became CEO in 1969.

His Stage One exercise was done on a global scale. He flew the wings off the company plane, flying to Saudi Arabia, Canada, South Africa; every place Mobil went, so did he. I went with him once to the Beaufort Sea and the Valdez terminal in Alaska. He ran on "Mobil time"; we showed up for everything 10 minutes early. He ran his company the same scheduled, fast-paced way.

He took his Stage One indoctrination in stride, but it wasn't easy. He had the gasoline crisis to handle, and he bought Montgomery Ward, an unhappy attempt to diversify. So he had his hands full.

As a strong, attractive CEO of one of the largest companies in the world, Warner was an immediate target for outside directorships. He began with AT&T, American Express, and Chemical Bank. He later added three more.

None of this kept him from enjoying himself. An avid eight handicapper, he played golf on weekends and was a popular outing guest.

I asked him how he managed such an active program. "First, I always gave Mobil top priority," he replied. "Unless things were on schedule there, I did not take any outside activities. And second, I had a strong COO and an efficient staff."

Warner never swung all the way into Stage Three; he was having too full an experience combining stages One and Two. He did, however, get involved in big issues; he simply kept the involvement in balance with his corporate work and other activities. He participated in the Business Roundtable and the Business Council. He crusaded in Washington for fair legislation for the energy industry. He raised money for Princeton, his alma mater. And he became a director of the Mayo Clinic.

Most prominently, in the famous Mobil advertisements on the Op-Ed page of *The New York Times*, he and his company spoke out on critical matters that affected his company, his industry, and his country.

This sophisticated CEO was always in control of his company, yet he found time to make a personal phone call or jot a note to friends. He was a superior leader, an outstanding and independent outside director, and a vital citizen. He had the staying power to be an effective CEO of one of the world's largest companies for 17 years.

William H. Wendel, former CEO, Carborundum Company. I worked for the Carborundum Company in Niagara Falls from 1961 to 1967, first as vice-president of marketing and then as a group vice-president in charge of five operating divisions. I reported directly to Wendel for a year when he was COO and for five years when he was CEO. After that I was in close enough contact with him to see how he handled his CEO obligations and opportunities.

As the heir apparent and as a longtime employee of Carborundum, a manufacturer of abrasives and high-performance ceramics, Wendel was a known quantity to his company long before he became CEO. He had visited its facilities worldwide and knew many of its several thousand employees.

Despite this familiarity, when Wendel became CEO, he responded as though recruited from outside. He revisited and re-met. He spoke to groups about his plans for change. He made it clear that he was in love with his company and his job, that exciting times were ahead, and that everyone had a wide-open opportunity to participate.

He mounted a host of new programs. He reorganized the company (which I liked because I got a group vice-presidency), and he made a number of significant acquisitions. He intensified a diversification program into related areas of technology, reducing dependence upon the mature abrasives industry. He expanded the company's global presence so that more than half of its revenues came from foreign sources. And he installed one of the first IBM 360 systems for corporatewide inventory control. Every facet of the business bore his mark. In his first five years, sales and profits rose by more than 50 percent.

Wendel was an orderly person, a planner, and a communicator. He let his board and staff know what he wanted and kept them informed. He also balanced his outside activities with his job. He went on outside boards but considered them an extension of his own board chairmanship: what could he learn that would help him do a better job? He organized a sweeping program to rebuild Niagara Falls, his headquarters city. Again, he believed that program was an integral part of his overall CEO job.

He was CEO of Carborundum for 15 years. During that time no one questioned who was in charge. Wendel loved setting up plans and had the staying power to make them come true. He had the support of his board, he was a productive member of the business and local communities, and he enjoyed his job.

John F. Welch Jr., CEO, General Electric Company. I ran across Jack Welch for the first time in 1975 at an executive seminar in Mexico. I was CEO of F. & M. Schaefer, and he was a 40-year-old vice-president in charge of General Electric's Pittsfield, Massachusetts, operations. He was a spirited, brash participant in the discussions, but right on the beam. I thought he was exciting and smart. I still do.

In my years as a CEO watcher, I have never seen a chief executive have such an impact on a large company so quickly and then continue that intensity as long as Welch has. He is changing GE's working culture, has made major acquisitions (not all successful), has redefined the GE product and market map, and has created a new vision of what GE can and will be under his leadership. People who work with him say that he learns from his experiences, a trait some CEOs never acquire.

Welch has been immersed in Stage One for nearly a decade,

and he maintains a full-court press. He travels incessantly, goes to multitudinous meetings, chairs his board with vigor, and gets involved in all kinds of transactions and programs. On top of this, he sends hundreds of handwritten notes and makes hundreds of phone calls.

A GE policy restricts its executives—other than the CEO—from serving on outside boards until just before their retirement. Welch has eschewed outside directorships for himself as well.

But Welch knows how to mingle with his fellow CEOs. He meets regularly with his outside directors and other chief executives. And he goes on enough golf dates to keep his handicap down. He knows his way around Washington and is prominent in the Business Roundtable. He attends a few conferences each year and belongs to a couple of prestigious clubs.

I asked him if he could imagine adjusting his personal plan to move into a broader version of stages Two and Three. "I'm trying to do what I think the CEO of GE should be doing—working as hard as I can to make this a great, profitable, growing, global company," he answered. "I've still got too many things to do and too little time to do them. Someday, maybe, I'll adjust my priorities and add a few more outside activities, but not now."

He's having fun, has a vision for his company, and has the staying power to finish up one of the biggest jobs in the world.

THE VERY FIRST CITATION PRODUCT
TO GO UP IN THE AIR WASN'T A BUSINESS JET.

Before the first Citation ever rolled off the line, we built the first service center dedicated exclusively to maintaining the aircraft.

Now, nearly 2,000 Citations later, there are Citation Service Centers located 45 minutes apart throughout the contiguous United States, and Authorized Citation Service Stations around the world.

When you own a Citation, we're here to take care of the aircraft so the aircraft and you can do what you do best. Take care of business.

THE SENSIBLE CITATIONS

Cessna
A Textron Company

Chapter Six

GETTING ADVICE

e can't all be world-acclaimed high achievers like Warner, Wendel, and Welch. But we *can* try to get the advice we need to keep our jobs and our companies moving. Yet one of the most difficult problems a CEO faces in any stage is finding the right mentors.

Self-appointed advisers are a dime a dozen. Everybody wants to get into the act of advising you.

CEOs do it. Lee Iacocca, Victor Kiam, David Mahoney, and even Donald Trump have written (or paid someone to write) their autobiographies, sprinkling them with advice for CEOs. (I hope you didn't pay attention too closely.)

Writers do it, especially those who work for *Business Week*, *Forbes*, *Fortune*, and the *Harvard Business Review*. I do it. And the books of Peter Drucker, Tom Peters, and Laurence Peter offer a never-ending stream of counsel.

Professors almost make a profession out of it. Warren Bennis, Rosabeth Moss Kanter, Jeffrey Sonnenfeld. They not only write, they also speak at seminars, conferences, and management meetings.

Consultants *do* make it a profession. You can get compensation advice from Sibson, economics assistance from Brookings, and full service from McKinsey. If you need to know how to handle your pensions, environmental programs, or office layouts, there's a consultant for you.

Some of the most strident are lawyers, lenders, investment bankers, accountants, advertising agencies, and public relations firms. Occasionally in error but never in doubt, they happily accept high fees to tell you what to do and how to do it.

Your shareholders advise you about dividends, South Africa, the environment, and your compensation. Some are just gadflies and exhibitionists who show up and off at annual meetings. But others you need to take seriously. Institutional investors, for example, are beginning to organize proxy fights and are asking for board representation.

Often the CEO can adapt the counsel from all these sources to his special circumstances; the problem is wading through the chaff. Much of the advice is impersonal and remote. Much is specialized and theoretical. Some is conflicting and contradictory. And qualified advisers are hard to find.

Still, CEOs can benefit from talking through their personal plan with a carefully chosen, knowledgeable, and objective adviser.

The logical place to look for an adviser is the board of directors. If you begin to spend too much time on outside activities and too little on company operations, why not ask the board to redirect or alert you? Doesn't the board have the authority and isn't that their responsibility?

Would that it were that simple.

Boards are becoming more aware of their power, especially when hiring and firing the CEO. A decade or so ago, a chief executive was rarely deposed. Now the "Who's News" column in *The Wall Street Journal* regularly reports the "early retirement for personal reasons" of another CEO.

So the working relationship between the CEO and his board is highly variable and delicately tuned to the changing nuances of the business. Being your adviser can sometimes conflict with the continuing series of tasks a board has to perform.

Still, beneath the surface of routine administrative board duties, the outside directors are constantly evaluating your performance as CEO, although their assessment isn't expressed in words.

This should not surprise a CEO. Though it's unlikely that the board will have an agenda item labeled "Evaluation of the CEO," there are at least six times when it is going on. And anticipating those times may give you an opportunity to ask for advice.

In the first year of your appointment. You are still on probation as the board formalizes and interprets your mandate. If it wishes to limit you—for instance, by curtailing the number of outside boards you go on and when—this is the time it will set those limits.

When management succession is discussed. This may involve the appointment of a potential successor as COO or vice-chairman, or it may be in recognition of your impending retirement date. At any rate, it forecasts a potential change in your work habits.

When your compensation is changed. The Organization and Compensation Committee normally reviews the CEO's compensation package each year and recommends changes to salary, bonus, stock options, and benefits.

When the strategic plan is finalized. The board wants to see how your abilities fit your vision of the company's future. Do you have the staying power to cope with the projected changes? To a director your personal plan and the corporate plan are the same.

When the Committee of the Board meets. Not all boards have such a committee, but the number is increasing. This committee usually has the responsibility for appraising the flow of information to directors, meeting and agenda formats, directors' compensation and pensions, and, sometimes in conjunction with the Nominating Committee, the makeup of the board and performance of its directors.

When the board has private sessions. Many boards put a regular time on each agenda for the outside directors to meet alone. You can bet that the main topic of conversation is you.

Most boards don't have heart-to-heart chats with their CEOs until problems have arisen and it is too late to do much about them. But one way to encourage discussion between a board and its CEO is to formalize a procedure to do so. A controversial technique is to use contracts, renewable every three to five years. Some CEOs feel a contract makes them conditional CEOs; others prefer a gentleman's agreement. However, a contract provides a specific opportunity to discuss not only your past but your future.

There is a world of difference between having the board ask to monitor your performance and having you ask it to do so.

When you and the board, or a few of its outside directors, develop a dialogue, you can learn what the board expects in terms of quantifiable performance and how it expects you to respond to its questions and suggestions. You and your board can talk freely about your rapport with your managers, your development program for young executives, your communication philosophy, your willingness to volunteer information, your acceptance of criticism, and your methods for balancing inside and outside activities.

"The CEO can keep his balance," explains Pierson M. "Sandy" Grieve, the 64-year-old CEO of Ecolab, a specialty chemicals and services company in St. Paul, "if he is willing to share not only his vision but his problems and his mistakes with those of his board and management team, who can offer helpful and candid counsel. The antidote is to ask for truth from people who care enough to tell him when he is not wearing any clothes."

Will M. Storey, executive vice-president and CFO of American President Companies Limited, a shipping company in Oakland, California, is not as optimistic. Said Storey, "Few directors can play the dual role of challenging critic and quiet counselor. What the CEO needs is an 'ego-buster' who will periodically bring him back to reality."

Still, candid discussions between CEOs and their boards are more common than ever before. Except on rare occasions, the motivation to establish this candor has to come from the CEO himself. The remote or insecure chief executive may ultimately get corrective criticism and direction from his board, but the discussions will never be as harmonious as they would be if he initiates them.

Dwight Minton of Church & Dwight is impressive in the way he brings things to his board. He has the experience and the security to say, "Here's a problem we are running into. I don't yet have all of the facts put together—and I'm a long way from having a management recommendation. I hope to be ready by our next meeting. In the meantime, I would like to have your input." When I was on his board, Minton was impeccable in discussing his personal stewardship with his Organization and Compensation Committee. He would also ask for a reaction to perquisite changes, internal management moves, outside board invitations, and any other activities that could affect his company time. As a result his board and committee meetings were positive and participatory.

More often than not the CEO in search of a mentor is able to find a senior member or two on his board who can be helpful. On my board at Schaefer, John Howard Laeri, a former vice-chairman of Citicorp, was an excellent counselor. He helped me rearrange the board, sell vital policy changes, and cope with difficult issues. He also influenced my thinking about outside activities, particularly my decision to join the St. Regis Paper board. He seldom came to see me but was always receptive to my visits. Because of his advice I acted more confidently as CEO and later became a better outside director.

Harry C. Stonecipher, 56, told of being recruited as CEO of Sundstrand Corporation, a manufacturer of aircraft and aerospace equipment in Rockford, Illinois: "Coming into a company that had suffered through a defense contract scandal and lost credibility with its people and customers, I needed all the help I could get. I found it in our former vice-chairman, now retired; I retain him as an invaluable consultant and adviser. He knows the background, the people, and the relationships. With his understanding, I can handle critical issues with greater sensitivity."

A CEO is sometimes wise enough to think through his needs for a mentor early in his tenure. I asked W. Houston Blount, the chairman and former CEO of Vulcan Materials Company, a construction materials company in Birmingham, Alabama, about his experiences. "One of the things I set out to do was to build a strong and independent board," said Blount, 70. "Whenever I began to veer off from running the company full blast, the board set me straight. Or I would talk to my brother, who was CEO of Blount Inc. And I also enjoyed having discussions with my predecessor. But it all started with getting a top-quality board to begin with."

In smaller companies where the chief executive has control, he can bring outsiders in to counsel him. Daniel S. Jones, 53, CEO of Newsbank, an electronic publishing company, explained: "Now that we have over 300 employees in three locations, I have to give a lot more thought to the time I spend on personal projects and outside affairs. That's one of the reasons I established an advisory board of three outside directors—to help me plan my work load effectively. I can't afford to get out of control in any one of the three stages."

Sometimes a CEO has a built-in mentor. Cyril C. Baldwin Jr. consults his executive committee chairman, Arthur I. Mendolia, the 75-year-old cofounder of Cambrex Corporation.

"Mendolia and I have been partners for nearly 20 years," said Baldwin. "At least 100 times a year, the two of us would take a noontime walk in a small park in Bayonne, New Jersey, and talk about our business—our problems, our hopes, our future alternatives. When I became CEO, I continued the business and personal relationship. I come to independent conclusions and make independent decisions, but the privilege of talking things through first with an experienced, intelligent man like Mendolia is hard to beat."

Often you simply do not feel secure going to your board or you do not have an *éminence grise*. This happens when the board is family-, predecessor-, or investor-controlled or when you have just not had the opportunity to reshape the board. It doesn't mean, however, that you must be bereft of counseling sources. You can find an old friend, a former professor, a senior business associate outside the company, or occasionally a paid consultant you have come to trust.

Although I'm wary about using paid professionals as personal advisers (I'm afraid they'll tell me only what they think I want to hear), many consultants have been of great help to CEOs. Here are a few examples.

Charles Krause is a management consultant in Milwaukee. He specializes in developing strategic plans for about 100 clients. Most are CEOs of privately or closely held companies with less than $100 million in revenues, although several are CEOs of not-for-profit institutions. In talking about these relationships, Krause said, "Because my clients are predominantly from smaller cities or from smaller companies, they have not usually built a network of people to talk to and so are most responsive to what I would call 'mentoring.'

"When I work out strategic plans for them, I usually try to help them think about outside activities. I urge them to add outsiders to their boards and, in turn, to go on boards themselves. Mostly I try to put them in touch with other CEOs with whom they can discuss mutual problems."

Stanley R. Klion, who was vice-chairman of the management consulting group of Peat, Marwick, Mitchell, described a pertinent case: "A new CEO asked me to help him with the preparation of a long-term succession plan, identifying key individuals and establishing developmental programs. He was determined that his successor would be more carefully selected and better trained than he was. These discussions led to a series of talks that spanned a dozen years and constituted a continuing appraisal of his personal program well beyond the single issue of succession."

Newly recruited CEOs have special problems. They do not have a coterie of friends and supporters within the company. They rarely know the board. Yet they must act fast.

"I often start off knowing many of the directors better than the CEO does, so I can help him with his board organization approach," said Thomas Neff of Spencer Stuart. "Al-

1989

Some CEOs are uneasy seeking counsel from the board, but Cyril C. Baldwin Jr. (left) of Cambrex Corporation welcomes the advice of his executive committee chairman, Arthur I. Mendolia.

◆

so, over the first few years, I will often help a new CEO recruit a few executives. When I meet with him at those times, I can be a useful sounding board as he ponders outside boards and other elements of his personal plans."

A spouse often offers excellent counsel. I know. I have always talked through business problems with my wife. By acting as a good listener, she helps me get my alternatives in order. And by asking questions, such as, "What would happen if you say no?" or "Is this something you should defer until next year?", she encourages me to seek more information and to verify suspect data.

She also keeps our discussions confidential. And I can be completely candid about my fears, doubts, and mistrusts. She has known me for many, many years, so I do not have to explain my values or principles. She is particularly sensitive to my overbooking and any symptoms of excess. Some of the time she is necessarily subjective, but she is more often uncannily objective. She keeps me in balance.

Walker Rast, the 57-year-old CEO of Keyes Fibre Company, a packaging firm in Norwalk, Connecticut, also consults his wife. "My wife is unusually perceptive in judging people, much better than I am," explained Rast. "She sees business and people from a different perspective, and so I pay attention to her reactions and observations."

Does this mean that I am urging CEOs everywhere to postpone making business decisions until they talk with their spouses? Of course not. There are wives who have never discussed business with their husbands, who do not care about the goings-on at the office or in the boardroom, and who have a distorted view of what a CEO's job can and should encompass.

On the other hand, to an increasing degree CEO wives are becoming more business oriented than ever before. Turi Josefsen, an executive vice-president of U.S. Surgical Corporation, is married to Leon Hirsch, Surgical's CEO. Adele "Del" Donati, executive vice-president of Houbigant Perfume, is married to Enrico Donati, Houbigant's CEO. When James E. Fuchs, CEO of Fuchs, Cuthrell & Company, became ill prior to a meeting of the Management Policy Council, Anne Sutherland Fuchs, his wife and the publisher of *Vogue*, planned and chaired the meeting. When David Gardner was president of the University of California, his wife held the title Associate of the President. When she died in 1991, Gardner announced his resignation.

I am sure that there are hundreds of similar examples, just

as I am sure that in hundreds of cases the spouse has had a negative influence. Either way a CEO spouse is a force to be reckoned with. As CEO spouses gain more and broader work experience, their influence will intensify. Notice the Clinton-Gore campaign.

Still, even when the CEO has talked with his board, his senior counselors, his consultants, and his wife, the decisions and responsibilities remain his own. As my hard-bitten CEO friends will say, "So what else is new?"

PERHAPS THE MOST IMPORTANT THING WE BUILD AT THIS CESSNA PLANT IS HUMAN POTENTIAL.

A year ago, this Cessna worker was considered unemployable. Lacking skills and education, she and her children lived on welfare checks.

But a new program, initiated by Cessna Aircraft Company, changed all that. The program provides job training for the undereducated. It gives each person a basic skill, a means to make a living, and a source of pride.

Graduates of the program now build high-quality parts for Cessna and, at the same time, something even more valuable. Better lives for themselves.

THE SENSIBLE CITATIONS

Cessna
A Textron Company

Chapter Seven

LOOKING AHEAD

The CEO's job is tough. He works long hours, often under severe pressure. His performance is always being measured, and, if his company is public, every quarter the press publishes his scorecard. His is a high-risk job; unless a CEO performs well, he's in danger of losing his job before mandatory retirement.

CEOs who have done a good job and who do stay in office deserve a reward—and they usually get it in the form of a good pension, exercisable stock options, and respect from the business community. But there should be more to it.

An integral part of your personal plan while you are a Stage Three CEO should be devoted to your life after retirement. I have seen CEOs who do nothing but say, "Oh, I'll travel or fish. Don't worry about me." That is not the way to do it.

A byproduct of my discussion with both active and retired CEOs is a consensus that earlier and more effective personal planning is crucial. One former CEO told me, "You ought to have a Stage Four called 'Discovering Yourself After Retirement.'"

To be sure, retirement planning for a large number of CEOs has little or nothing to do with continuing involvement in business or a specific activity. Retirement simply consists of buying a resort home in a warm climate and spending the rest of their lives golfing, sailing, painting, reading, etc. Maybe they stay on a couple of boards and dig their suits out of the closet once or twice a month to attend meetings, but that's about all.

More and more, however, I am finding CEOs who feel the way I did when my CEO term was over. I wanted to get started on a second career and had no thought of retiring. The word was not in my vocabulary.

I like the way David T. Kearns, 62, did it while he was CEO of Xerox. His great outside interest was in education, and he became something of an authority in the field. He accepted an appointment to serve on the President's Council for Education and also co-wrote a book. Because of this commitment to an agenda, he was able to be selective in choosing what else he did; he could focus his attention and fend off well-meaning solicitations. When he retired early to become deputy secretary of Education in the Bush administration, he topped off an admirable career that bridged both public and private life.

Not everyone can retire the way Kearns did, but many CEOs have found a special activity unusually rewarding. Others have applied their energies to a charity, a trade association, a museum, or a hobby.

James Curtis of Milliman & Robertson is an excellent golfer active in several golf associations. As a part of his personal plan and with clearance from his board, he has become a member of the executive committee of the USGA—and that will be the platform of his retirement program.

In 1980, three years before his retirement, Donald Seibert, CEO of J.C. Penney Company, went to his board with a dual plan. He had a carefully worked out succession plan and a phase-in schedule. At the same time, Seibert offered a personal program that included increased participation in community affairs, more involvement in the industry trade association, and beginning work on a book about ethics.

As chief executive of Xerox, David T. Kearns joined the President's Council for Education, building expertise that led President Bush to appoint him U.S. deputy secretary of Education.

◆

I keep running into retired CEOs who have found exciting new lives. As I've mentioned, Thomas Carroll took a post as CEO of the International Executive Service Corps after retiring as CEO of Lever Brothers. He is in a position to offer overseas assignments in developing countries to hundreds of other retiring executives, many of whom were CEOs. William F. May, former CEO of American Can, now a financial services company called Primerica, became dean of New York University Business School. Hicks B. Waldron, former CEO of Avon Products, heads up a firm specializing in the recruitment of outside directors. Dukes Wooters, once CEO of Cotton Incorporated, a research and promotional company for the U.S. cotton industry, now works full time as a merchant banker. Robert J. Callander, former vice-chairman of Chemical Banking Corporation, is joining me as an executive-in-residence at Columbia Business School.

Not all of these moves were planned, but they illustrate the rewarding activities available to a retiring CEO. Rather than waiting for a Stage Four career, why not include some retirement thinking in your personal plan?

As I talk with my Columbia Business School students about becoming CEOs, I try to anticipate what corporations are going to look like in the future. Most companies will be global with a complex network of joint ventures, alliances, and licensing arrangements. The hierarchical way of management life is gone in many companies. Electronic communication and computerization are speeding up all processes.

Boards of directors are behaving much more independently. It is no longer surprising to see a CEO ousted or a company redirected. Insider boards and beholden directors are increasingly rare. Job security for CEOs will be even more tenuous.

With all of this global and corporate change, CEOs will also change. A personal plan that anticipates and capitalizes upon these changes will become even more important.

I suggest to my students, however, that many things will be the same. Despite their M.B.A.'s and extensive executive training programs, they will come into their new posts with more to learn than they know. Like the CEOs before them, they will have to learn on the job.

I tell them to recognize early the definable stages of CEO life—and that each stage can offer an opportunity for better performance and increased job satisfaction.

In Stage One, when you discover yourself, your power, and the glory of running your company, you cannot afford to become so insulated that you fail to learn from your peers and from the world outside the corporate sphere.

In Stage Two, when you discover your fellow CEOs, you must take care not to be engulfed by their exciting diversions. Like seasoning, a certain amount adds to the taste; too much ruins the dish.

In Stage Three, when you discover the outside world, you

are perhaps most vulnerable to upsetting the balance between your corporate and personal roles. You see retirement ahead and are in danger of losing touch with your people.

The hardest job in the corporate world is that of CEO. You are responsible for your company's people, its profits, and its future. You are under continuous pressure from both inside and outside forces to do what is "good for you and for the company." When you have a personal plan, you can keep your balance. With just a bit of luck, you are then in position to make one more discovery: the best job in the world is that of the CEO.

EVERY 22 SECONDS, SOMETHING QUITE UNEVENTFUL HAPPENS SOMEWHERE IN THE WORLD.

A Citation takes off or lands safely every 22 seconds. The aircraft's safety record is even more remarkable considering there are nearly 2,000 of them in the world's largest fleet of business jets.

In aviation, the Collier Trophy is the highest tribute to excellence. The trophy was created in 1911, but 75 years went by before it was given to honor a business aircraft company.

The Citation's unmatched safety record is why that company is Cessna.

THE SENSIBLE CITATIONS

Cessna
A Textron Company

Additional Copies

To order additional copies of *Pressure Points*
for friends or colleagues, please write to
The Chief Executive Press, Whittle Books,
333 Main St., Knoxville, Tenn. 37902.
Please include the recipient's name, mailing
address, and, where applicable, title,
company name, and type of business.

For a single copy, please enclose a check
for $13.95, plus $2.90 for postage and han-
dling, payable to The Chief Executive Press.
Discounts are available for orders of 10 or
more books. If you wish to order by phone,
call 800-284-1956.

Also available, at the same price,
are the previous books from
The Chief Executive Press:
Getting the Job Done by Kenneth L. Adelman
and *What Are You Worth?* by Graef S. Crystal.

Please allow two weeks for delivery.
Tennessee residents must add 8¼ percent sales tax.